THE EPITOME OF

Perseverance

A JOURNEY TO HER CROWN...

A Memoir

ERIKA R. PAIGE

IMPERFECT PAIGE
PUBLISHING, LLC

Look for these books also written by author Erika R. Paige and self-published by: Self-Published by: Imperfect Paige Publishing, LLC

GiGi's Glimpse of Virtual Learning
Zeke's Great Imagination
The Epitome of Perseverance: A Journey to Her Crown...A Memoir

Printed in the United States of America.
For more information, or a book feature, please contact:
publishpaiges@gmail.com
http://www.imperfectpaigepublishing.com
Some photography by: Lee Richardson
ISBN - Hardcover: 978-1-7365042-2-2

PERSEVERANCE (NOUN)

Persistence and continued effort in doing something despite difficulty or delay in achieving success. Synonyms: persistence, tenacity, determination, resolve, resolution, resoluteness, staying power, purposefulness, firmness of purpose, patience, endurance, application, diligence, sedulousness, dedication, commitment, doggedness, pertinacity, assiduity, assiduousness, steadfastness, tirelessness, indefatigability, stamina, intransigence, obstinacy, Sitzfleisch continuance, perseveration

---

TABLE OF CONTENTS

PREFACE

Authoring a book is much like anticipating the arrival of a baby. I thank God for blessing me with two children, and unveiling this process reminded me of when I was "nesting" with them. Most authors can relate to the idea that drafting a book can be symbolically like delivering a baby. Spending hours upon hours trying to choose just the right words to say to welcome the very thing that has occupied a huge portion of your time. The writer's block, lack of sleep, and determination to publish a best seller and become the best author I can be. Upon becoming a new mother, I learned how to swaddle my baby, which was essential for their comfort. Creating a soothing environment for the baby to rest. Once my babies became warm and swaddled in their blankets, they would no longer lose control of their extremities, giving them a sense of stability and comfort. Oftentimes, they would even scare themselves with the instability. A mother's love is the purest form of unconditional love. It is her job to teach compassion and fearlessness, which shape and mold who they become. So, as I swaddle up this gift and put this baby to bed, I'm at peace with releasing the hurt, the burdens, the trauma, and the generational curses that have impacted my life. Now, I can deliver it right to your doorstep, doting with joy but exhausted by the journey while healing from the shame of it all. Yet the truth shall set you free. Guided with a little mustard seed faith, sprinkled with the luck of the draw decisions, a little unwise judgment, and topped heavily with perseverance, I am here to share this memoir, journey, and testimony. So, whether it is by coincidence or divinely inspired. "The Epitome of Perseverance, A Journey to Her Crown is a manifestation of strength. After several attempts to title this book, I knew it was confirmation after I noticed the initials of my name were coincidentally the acronym for this book. The Epitome of Perseverance is not about how much you can manage before breaking but about how much you can endure after brokenness.

CHAPTER 1

❧

DEAR PERSEVERANCE

"There is no greater agony than bearing an untold story inside you." – Dr. Maya Angelou

I am thankful for God's blessings and for giving me the fortitude to accept the suffering it takes to persevere. From what seemed like an experiment gone wrong to a one-of-a-kind skillset. From the moment my mother's contractions started and to the point where she nearly gave birth to me sitting on a toilet, it seemed God had decided you should endure a bit more pain before you made it to the hospital. The birthing plan was not as expected as I erupted through my mother's womb, making my debut as a healthy baby girl in the middle of July. Little did I know that my unusual fate was just around the corner. As I reflect on a cascade of untold stories, unraveled at a consistent pace, it becomes clear that each one has left a permanent mark on my existence. Despite the complications presented since my inception, the act of perseverance has been a part of my life, just like a mother giving birth to her child. You have got to do what you have got to do to get through it, especially in hard times. I became almost dependent upon relying on the difficult strength, but I welcomed it with open arms. I would like to think that a magnetic force runs in my bloodline, but the critical path method of my life seemed predestined by an abyss of obstacles, one after another. While time is always of the essence, I have learned to trust the divine order and witness the transformation of life's highs and lows. I have learned that it is the love of oneself who speaks positive affirmations, who can endure such obstacles and still offer hope to someone else despite the circumstances. You are not alone. "Nevertheless, she persisted," is a profound quote used as an analogy because I will never be less, nor will I settle for less when life is full of possibilities. I vow to no longer have self-imposed limitations on myself to appease others' expectations, just for their own comfort. As the queen that I am, my royalty is reflective of the victories won and validated by God's presence over my life. With all my imperfections, flaws, and sins, I am still chosen to share my story at this very moment, invoking vulnerabilities that are a part of my healing process as multifaceted and full of layers. My focus is to continuously aim to be a better me. Personal growth is an objective every single day. So, as I walk in my purpose to encourage others to stand by their truth, and whether there were tragedies or tumultuous times that may have happened, when one is free, the burdens completely fall. Allow yourself to live a more fruitful life with unexpected blessings. I trust readers will soak their emotions into these circumstances and recognize the state of mind of one who is releasing negative energy while healing at the same time. It brings me comfort to know God grants me the perseverance needed to get through my turmoil. With me forming my testimonies and whispering words of wisdom while keeping my mind away from the insanities of life. I would not be here to tell my story had I not experienced these situations. So, as I embark on this memoir and the journey that has led me to my self-proclaimed crown, I've longed to share my story of loss, lack, and neglect with the world. I release the embarrassment and embrace the situations that were out of my control, the freak of nature accidents, and metaphorically, the survival of the fittest environments I've endured. During those times of defeat, I would resort to my knees with my little mustard seed faith, crying for change. It is the most daunting instance of experiences that have led to a change. I have witnessed when God comes through. The Epitome of Perseverance is an acronym for my initials and in reference to all the life-changing, traumatic events. As you read this book, pay attention to the experiences that have tested my faith, influenced my view of love and the things that impacted my role as a mother. Also, consider the situations that have either built or weakened trust among friends, as well as strained family relationships. There are critical moments that reveal heartache and dysfunction, which shift the mindset. For instance, overcoming toxic people will transform your life. It's like detoxifying your body; and as each day passes, it brings better energy. Unfortunately, at some point, I became tolerant of abandonment, abuse, betrayal, and isolation. However, if you do not stand for something, you'll fall for anything. So, when I am down, I don't stay down and refuse to walk into a room with my head down. While energized by my dear perseverance, I managed to stay on the right path to triumph. Peeling back each layer, exposing the endurance of each emotion in my ever-changing environment.

⨳

CHAPTER 2

I AM WHO I AM

"I spent much of my childhood listening
to the sound of striving."
– Michelle Obama

Aname can be worth a thousand words and countless conversations. And in the next few chapters, you will discover that those difficult conversations are the most important ones to have. Do you believe that your name is reflective of your personality? If I am just speaking for myself, then absolutely! Better yet, does your name reflect your identity? I would like to think that you are what you respond to, but after further research, I learned that our names form our identities. A first name has the power to influence one's personality, love life, and destiny. The name Erika means eternal ruler, forever powerful, and in biblical terms, it means sole ruler or monarch. I even researched down to the Nordic root of my name, which symbolizes one who is alone or unique. For this purpose, I have associated myself with being a child of the King. Thanks be to God; I shine brightest when I am demonstrating what real love is all about, especially when God has a hand in it. Being the King's kid means learning about selfless love from the Master Himself and then sharing it with others, whether they understand it or not. "We love Him because he first loved us." (1 John 4:19). That's why this child of the King has self-proclaimed her crown. But what is interesting is whether your name means enough for you to change it. In an uncanny predicament that was beyond my control. Throughout my adolescent years and into adulthood, I consistently misspelled my first name, Erika, by using a C. Unbeknownst to me using the C in my name wasn't accurate. So, I legally changed my name so it would match, and since my birth certificate would be the most accurate, I re-learned how to write my name using the letter k. In retrospect, God changed Abram's name to Abraham, Sarai's to Sarah, Jacob to Israel, and Simon to Peter. Through those names, God granted them new beginnings, new hopes, and new blessings which I humbly receive. Although differentiations in the name were becoming a nuisance when it came to personal matters, nothing superseded a birth certificate. So, it was easier to change it to the name it was meant to be. Modifying all government documents to reflect the same spelling of my name was the symbolism of becoming the woman I wanted to be. It was the fresh start that I needed as a twenty-something-year-old woman in a new city. The magic of new beginnings can reset your life in the right direction. I quickly became familiar with everything new, including my signature, while learning to leave the old name behind. Certainly, the change of my name was for consistency's sake; however, I am who I am, and my name and where I come from can no longer be an unsolved mystery among my peers. The mystery of an absentee mother hurt me, but I didn't have time for that; I had to mother myself. Whether it was for school activities, shopping for clothes, or just nurturing, life was difficult as a child, feeling like an old ragamuffin. My dysfunctional family had me struggling with identity issues. It wasn't until I was an adult that I learned about my maternal history. I saw life differently through the lens of a child whose mother had an illness. She suffered from Huntington's disease, a rare disease that affects the nerve cells in the brain, breaking down over time. Unfortunately, she missed the opportunity to raise her own children for most of my life. However, she gave birth to me, loved me, and was entitled to name me just as she desired. I am who I am, and coincidentally, named me after the infamous soap opera character 'Erika Kane' from "All My Children." Mommy was a faithful soap opera watcher and seemed to live vicariously through her favorite character, especially with all the drama. Undoubtedly, the show had its fair share of scandals and betrayals, but as crazy as it sounds, my life also has the propensity to emulate some of that drama. In this heartfelt memoir, I embark on a nostalgic journey down memory lane, delving deep into the corners of my past. As I embrace the therapeutic power of storytelling, I unravel the layers of my life, stitching together the moments that have shaped me into the person I am today. The connection of my middle name, Rose originated from my grandmother Rosalie. Most people called her Rosa for short. Although I have fond memories of her, she left my life when I was only about five years old. But the distinct memories are so surreal, like a running movie in my mind. Set in the nostalgic mid-eighties, with Stevie Wonder music playing fondly in the background "singing, I just called to say I love you." When my grandmother and I were apart, our phone conversations would entail singing that song to each other before we hung up. In fact, the song has brought tears to my eyes thinking of those times. In those early years, we seldom spent time apart; her home still sits in the Olney section of Philadelphia. The nostalgic vibes of heavy cigarette smoke and records spinning on her wooden turntable console are a photographic memory. This reminds me of a renowned quote: "A memory is a diary that we all carry around within us". However, my memories were not always bad, but they were not always good either. She had a mean streak to her persona but with a heart of gold. I guess you can say that trait passed down honestly. As a child I had so much independence, I was one of those kids who walked to the corner store alone to purchase Granny's cigarettes. The store clerk knew who I was as I placed a written note on the counter with the name of the cigarette brand she wanted. With the change, I would pick out my choice of penny candy, including Lemon heads, Boston baked beans, and Jawbreakers. However, it came with a price because what was next was the daunting task of getting my hair done. With the combination of cigarette smoke and the billowing cloud of hair grease burning from the straightening comb, our Saturday main event helped me become one hell of a creator at home with my own hair. Granny would wash, blow dry, hot-comb, and cornrow my hair as we watched Soul Train. My only downfall was being so tender-headed that Granny's patience would grow thin, and she would punish me with the comb. It was love and war in Granny's kitchen as her cuckoo clock chimed every hour, and I learned the act of endurance. Although I endured physical pain, my inner strength became tolerant of distress at such an early age. I even grew up ridiculed by classmates for having thick, untamed hair. Other kids would call me names like 'wild' and Crème of Nature' just because I lacked the basic upkeep a girl should have. Ironically, I endured those awful hair experiences and eventually built the confidence to make passive income as an adult by doing sew-ins, cornrows, braids, relaxers, and color for other people. It is simply a gift from God, and for that, I am thankful. Even considering the past traumas that have triggered intense emotions, I have claimed power over that trauma, and it has helped me move past it. Those traumas are who we are. They indirectly develop who we can become. One weekend, Granny had all three of her grandchildren. What seemed like a common event for any other grandmother, quickly that experience changed for her and us. It was a normal afternoon; we were playing outside when my brother popped our cousin in the eye with a rubber band. He must have gotten the rubber band from a local newspaper near the front steps. As a result, my cousin cried hysterically, and once Granny heard what happened, it was like walking the plank with her. I had nothing to do with it and feared the consequences for him. And although the scripture says, "Spare the rod spoils the child," it was the level of harm that was meant to teach my brother a lesson. Granny went to the basement staircase, where a row of thick leather dog collars and leashes hung. The collars were customized for her German Shepherds; she loved those dogs. When any of us got out of line, a whooping was exactly what we got, and we felt for each other. But that day was the last time she whooped any of us ever again. That was also the last day I would ever see her again. Granny despised my father, and that evening he returned to pick us up from her house. He saw that he had enough evidence to convince Philly PD, child protective services, and a judge that we were not safe with her. Insinuating that she would take her anger and disdain for my father out on his children. In the eyes of most people, seeing the lashes from a belt on a child reveals a story of its own. And I am certain it worked in Dad's favor based on serving in the Philadelphia Police Force. So, of course, the authorities would help a former "man in blue" protect his children. But it came with a price because I had my fair share of whooping's not just from Granny, but also from my dad too. Some were deserving, and some underserving this continued to impact me well into my adult years. Nevertheless, I am who I am. With all my imperfections, scars, and traumas, I am a black woman who is familiar with challenges and faces them head-on. I have learned to equip myself for battle when it pertains to my family. Even challenges with growing up under Dad's care, as it was not all that it was cracked up to be. In fact, Daddy's girl sounded much better than it really was. My reality was that I didn't get the gentle, loving care that I desired. Many days came with hunger pains, and the limitations on food were stressful. And the lack of essential clothing items just was not a priority for me. Now, don't get me wrong; that's the only father I have, and without him, I would not be here or be the woman I am today. And without the neglect, struggle, and oversaturation of tough love, I would not have listened to the sounds of striving. I can relate to Mrs. Obama's sentiment ever so clearly. To want for something so bad that you can almost taste it. For me, that was freedom. Freedom to live my life on my own terms, even if those terms left me secluded and isolated from the battles that came with dealing with family. As an adult, I analyzed myself through the lens of a child and it's clear that I was searching for a certain level of comfort and peace. As a child, I prayed for unconditional love from my family, but sometimes, the ridicule of my mistakes outweighed a peaceful outcome. When parents use tough love as part of a child's discipline experience, if not used carefully, it can backfire. It's a fact that children are extremely vulnerable to rejection, ridicule, criticism, and anger at home, so they deserve to grow up in a home environment of safety, acceptance, and warmth. Deep down, I was searching for genuine love from my dad that was not out of obligation. This little Tomboy at heart craved a different kind of fostering especially considering my mom's instability and my chaotic childhood. Yet, I am thankful for the discernment that has led me out of countless risky situations. Nowadays, it would be ideal to manage a child's vulnerabilities with a licensed counselor to help guide children through those abandonment feelings. My mental health as an adolescent was not analyzed and could have been assessed considering the behaviors I expressed. When you think your child is acting out, believe them. Unfortunately, in those days, sending a child to a psychologist in my community was unheard of unless something was significantly wrong. Instead, this little girl would wrap herself in a shell of my own. Skeptical of most adults, including those who have the same DNA. Trust is an act we all take for granted because it is not easy to reveal pieces of yourself to prove that you are trustworthy. Daddy was a churchgoing, God-fearing man who helped mold my spirituality. I spent many days and nights in the house of God, as my dad was a pillar in the community and an advocate for the students he mentored. At times, I was envious of the attention he gave his students. It wasn't unusual for a student to ring the doorbell, as many knew where we lived. As the local high school's basketball coach and founder of a basketball summer camp, he was a one-of-kind guy, generous with his time and money. His leadership in the church and in the community was admirable. However, the family structure at home needed some work. The instability was something that often took a toll on my childhood mental state and behavior, and to make matters worse, there was favoritism between my brother and me. This has caused a bit of sibling resentment since. My brother was two years older than me and manipulated situations to benefit him. I remember I was required to iron my brother's clothes claiming he couldn't do it as well as me. Instead of having a teaching moment with Dad's son, I had to iron his clothes for him as if I was the black Cinderella. Afterwards, the smirk on his face forced me to have enough contempt for him. The reality was that he was lazy, and he knew how to use his testosterone to get the support he needed. Could it have been easier for Dad to communicate and raise a boy versus a girl? I suppose so. Or was there favoritism because he was his namesake? Whatever it was, I was overlooked, and most days, felt ostracized. The mindset of a young girl is impressionable between the ages of ten and fifteen. As the only girl in the household, I was misunderstood, teased, bullied, and underrepresented. In the story of Queen Cleopatra, she had a sibling rivalry so cruel that they all succumbed to their deaths in defiance of her. The Queen of Egypt, also known as the Last Pharaoh, is just one example of royalty fighting for her respect. Cleopatra 's feud with her siblings resulted in all-out wars to maintain the throne of her kingdom. In a male-dominated household, how dare I be surprised that my sibling could wage war on me? Bullying in those days would be extreme times ten. It's the people you love the most that turn out to be the people you can trust the least. It was like he was determined to break my spirit down. He would often call me dumb and worthless and laugh at my weaknesses. My brother's lack of compassion was simply due to the lack of nurturing that comes from a mother. But other times, I think he was groomed to be the prodigal son. The namesake child was deeply favored, showered with excess attention, and applauded for their potential success. It was not uncommon for my intelligence to become the mockery of family and friends, serving as the main attraction for their amusement, as if I were utterly hopeless and lacked any trace of common sense. Ignoring my insecurities, my own father not only endorsed but also enjoyed my brother's comedic mockery. They seemed to be conspiring together, intentionally leaving me on the outskirts. Was the goal to break me down and make it difficult for me to achieve anything? Year after year, I constantly fought with my sibling and began to seek refuge at my next- door neighbor's house. At ten years old, it was my only recourse. My neighbor Bethany was my Caucasian sister from another mister. She was at least a decade older than me and quickly became my confidant, seeing firsthand the shortcomings that I dealt with at home. Her home became a place of protection, and I'm not sure if I would have survived without her presence at times. In fact, my love-hate relationship with my family members at home led me to run away more than once. The first time I ran away from home, I only went to a friend's house for just a few hours. No one even noticed I was gone. However, another time when I ran away from home, it put me in an uncompromising situation. I was only about thirteen years old in a situation that left me in a car with two strange young men. If it were up to them, they would have raped me. I cringed at the touch of more than one set of hands trying to touch my body. As curious as I was, I was still innocent and scared then. I screamed and elbowed my way out of the car. It seemed like I was running for my life in the darkness throughout Elmwood Park in Norristown. See, persevering is all about enduring or a show of resilience. It's about your ability to weather tough situations. Perseverance without hope for a change of situation can make one feel lost or left behind. It can turn one into a very bitter person. I had hoped that the tough situations wouldn't last forever, and that leaving home would be my last resort. Besides, our little family had its good times, surrounded by sports, church, and our family in inner-city Philly. Something was missing in our interactions, and that was the word "love." In fact, saying the word "I love you" was not common at all. I seem to believe that the lack of expression of love comes from the generational curse of slavery. Since my ancestors gave birth to children breeding purposes only for labor and not for raising. I suppose there was a sense of detachment, and the word love became displaced throughout many families. But thanks to hope and perseverance, things can change. Although Daddy was a fool for love as he made decisions based on creating a ready-made family. It took a toll on my emotions, especially when his relationships did not last. Too far in between did I have a place of belonging amongst my six stepmothers and their children. And although Daddy was an imperfect man and a father who built a stable life for us, he had his mistakes as well. My existence was like black Cinderella, especially with chores and lack of freedom to socialize outside school. My athletic ability was not good enough for the quality time I yearned for. Nevertheless, I would like to think that my dad did the best he could as a parent. And fortunately, our father-daughter relationship became much more pleasant once I became an independent adult. He had to learn how to love me the way I needed love, nurturing, and protection. I just wish I could have alleviated the brokenness if my dad had been open to real conversation. Conversations about the real world, who to trust and who not to. Instead, I was seeking attention in all the wrong places and not knowing how to distinguish the wrong kind of company. My choices of guys were not always worthwhile. However, there were lessons learned through different relationships, and getting through tough times seemed to be deal-breakers. Shortly after my eighteenth birthday, my dad scared me straight. As a teen, I relocated to Kinston, North Carolina from Pennsylvania, staying there from age sixteen to nineteen. But I spent most summers there as an adolescent. But a new start was exactly what I needed, as I attended the local high school for one year. I was the new kid from up north with a messed-up accent. I worked a part-time job at Bojangles and had a social life that was full of events. Basically, the deal that my dad and I agreed upon was that as long as my grades remained at an acceptable level, I could live independently in the family home. I enrolled at the community college and lived the life people envied. These times were great, meeting good friends and making memories. Including being one of the head cheerleaders for the LCC basketball team, my bestie Lesa and I were living the life. However, it came with making decisions to be with someone that cost me my freedom. I was mentally incarcerated at the thought of someone loving me the wrong way. The man I dated at the time was somewhat of forbidden fruit. Given that, no father wants to hear about their daughter dating, especially a man he did not approve of. But nothing could keep me from my man, and as a result, my dad and stepmother number three traveled from Pennsylvania to North Carolina without my knowledge arriving at about three in the morning. My boyfriend and I were asleep in bed together when Dad immediately woke us up and escorted my company out the front door. "How embarrassing?" I thought. However, while he was being shown the door, my evil stepmother and her microaggression instigated a fight. I mean, why did she think it was okay to take my sheets off the bed before spraying them with Lysol for her kids to sleep? Before I knew it, I blacked out and began swinging. I proceeded to grab a small mallet or hammer and strike her head. Throughout the commotion, my dad stumbled to the back room to break up the fight and ended up falling on us both. I immediately began packing my things to leave, and by the time I got to the front door Kinston's police arrived, ready to take me to jail. Although I didn't recall hitting her that badly with the hammer, my dad eventually pressed charges. And there I was, eighteen years old with my first and only run-in with the law. I spent an entire seventy-two hours with the general population at the county jail. I had never felt that kind of fear, abandonment, and heartbreak before. The person who should have been protecting me had sent me off to jail. Since it was a Friday night, I wasn't allowed to see a magistrate until Monday morning. On my first night there, I cried for hours. While I slept on the floor on a jail mattress, I had a surreal encounter with God. He told me, "Be strong", and I felt His presence. In the following days, I received encouragement from those who were there. "Sweet Pea" was the nickname they gave me. Those women knew I should not have been there, and a few of them even helped me get through it. I learned to be a confident card player, whether in Blackjack, Spades, Tunk, or Rummy 500. The next two days, I was able to take my mind off what happened. I was gathering the strength I needed to get through my court hearing. The day of my court hearing, I was clothed in an olive-green county jail jumper, handcuffed, and shackled at the ankles. And in preparation for my hearing the next day, I had my jail-mate braid my hair straight to the back. She had just beat me in cards for my cookies the night before. The next morning, I had nothing but faith on my side as I headed to court to represent myself. This was a battle I knew the Lord would fight for me. As I described exactly what happened that night to the judge. I explained how it was unfair for my father to come there unannounced. Although I was afraid of what could have happened because this was the first time I was in trouble with the law. I explained that my family was toxic and that my dad and his ex-wife had no relationship with me; it was a situation marked by jealousy and control. And just like that, I convinced the judge that I wasn't a menace to society. I had a job, attended college, and maintained good grades. As a result, he ruled in my favor. The judge gave me a time-served charge along with twelve months of probation. The judge made sure he mentioned to me that if I got into any more trouble, my next sentence wouldn't be so easy. That was the pivotal moment. I couldn't trust anyone again. I had no one else to turn to except the began abusing me. We began to live with each other shortly after my dad's run- in. Ultimately, I ceased all communications with my dad for more than a year and focused on working rotating shifts in the manufacturing industry. In between that time, he also ended another marriage, which was best in the long run. Once that marriage ended, my dad asked me to relocate back to Pennsylvania. I forgave my father, and our once misunderstood relationship began to mend, eventually growing better with time. For we all have sinned and come short of the glory of God." This scripture helped me overcome such pain. "Meaning that none of us are perfect, and we must grant each other a level of grace because that is what God gives us. Ironically, my dad and I became confidants; he, in me, and I, in him. It was like he finally respected me as an adult, and the toxic behaviors ended. The neglect I felt for so long seemed to be a thing of the past. I could finally see that dad wanted me to succeed, and in hindsight, maybe I was supposed to go through those struggles to prepare me for some of my hardest battles. If we did nothing else, we worshipped together just as I did as a kid who stayed in church three to five days a week and got involved in everything. I'm no Aretha Franklin or anything, but my father encouraged me to use my gift of singing for the Lord. He spontaneously requested a selection on any given Sunday. I was really young when my connection with God began to flourish. Before I turned fourteen, my amazing Mom Bee gifted me my very own Bible. It was green leather with my name engraved on the bottom. I cherished it and spent a lot of time reading it. It seems like even back then, they saw something special in me, something divinely inspired. During my early twenties, my dad and I embarked on countless church visits in and around the Philadelphia and Delaware area. Daddy helped mold my spirituality. While he preached, I would sing solos to support him, performing in various grassroots churches. At that time, he was pastoring a small church in Norristown. We were always accompanied by his close friend Sam who frequently joined us for fellowship. It was an incredible time of spreading love and faith wherever we went. Sam was one of the most talented individuals I have ever met. He said he used to play the saxophone for Patty LaBelle. But He also was gifted in other instruments including singing and playing the piano. He encouraged me and taught me to use my voice as my testimony because that's what he always did. Speaking of the darkest times in his life and then referencing how God brought him through them. And boy, he did have a story to tell! But my testimony was different and sometimes intimidating. I always had a level of fear when discussing my mom or the path my life had taken. In fact, I knew I was predestined, and sharing in this compelling moment revealed that I was set apart. And I believe that. Suppose all of life's struggles were meant to lead me into this beautiful chapter of my life.

CHAPTER 3

⟨✦⟩

A MOTHERLESS CHILD

"When a daughter loses a mother, she learns early that human relationships are temporary, that terminations are beyond her control, and her feelings of basic trust and security are shattered." – Hope Edelman

The sentiment "Motherless Child" stems from the African American spiritual that evokes the heart-wrenching tragedy of a child getting snatched from their mother's arms. My mom and I used to take the trolley in West Philadelphia near my dad's side of the family, off Lancaster Ave. While getting off the back door exit of the trolley, the driver must not have seen that I was not entirely off the train and proceeded to drive away a few yards down the track. My body was pinned between the middle of the train doors, with one arm in and the other arm out of the train. As my limp body moved inertly with fear, other passengers yelled at the driver for him to stop, all while my mom chased the trolley down to give him an old-school curse out. Unfortunately, I associate myself with the idea of that forcible separation. The sorrow that the old slavery song exhales is the same air I have inhaled since I was five years old. According to the Substance Abuse and Mental Health Services Administration, child traumatic survivors are more likely to have learning problems, increased use of mental or health services, involvement in juvenile justice systems, or long-term health problems. I will not say that I defied all the odds, but I did confront them. A girl growing up without a mother was not easy, and it was certainly unusual, but so was her disease. Huntington's disease continues to be an illness most people haven't heard of. The inherited condition contributes to nerve cells in the brain breaking down and worsening over time. An incurable disease that has affected not only my mother, but her brother, and her father, whom I never met. Word has it, he was in a mental hospital in Pennsylvania shortly after he returned from the war. The emotional effects of being a motherless child, a product of divorced parents, and the possibility of inheriting the very same disease that my mother, uncle, and grandfather succumbed to. It makes me wonder, is this my destiny as well? Maybe it was a good thing I got the runaround when I expressed this to the medical staff. It cost me over three hundred dollars when I went to see about getting tested. All to find out that I should have gone to a genetics doctor. I was so confused, asking myself who did I just see? I thought to myself, "oh, never mind!" I guess I'll never find out. Nevertheless, my parents were a dysfunctional couple who produced two children out of that crazy thing called love. But the reality is her illness was not allowing her to be the best parent she could be. In fact, I stopped living with my mother full-time at the age of five, and that is when the drama began. From then on, my father had custody of me while visitation rights were granted to my mother. Most times, we visited her while she resided in mental health halfway houses or local motels. We did arts and crafts together and played board games to spend time with her. Which always resulted in her not wanting to give us back. Her presence started to give me anxiety, and her hostile episodes would become embarrassing. During the end of a visitation one weekend, something in her mind just triggered her to be defiant while walking us to the car. Back in the eighties and nineties, my dad always had a big car. During this time, he had a navy-blue Cadillac Deville, the one with the large back window. His window was so big that I could fit my entire body in it. And that's exactly what I did as my mother held onto my brother's ankles through the window while my dad held my brother's upper torso. As these two adults played tug-of-war with my sibling, I cringed in the back window, and the impact of my childhood trauma had only just begun. I was in fear of my own mother. She was aggressive, had shaky body movements, and was unpredictable. Eventually, those visits got awkward, and visitations conveniently ended. Thereafter, I never got to see her at all, from the age of nine to nineteen. I seldom wonder if anyone had diagnosed her with Huntington's disease sooner; maybe she could have alleviated the struggles she had in life. Imagine having a misdiagnosis of schizophrenia, and the walls are crumbling down because you are losing your marriage, your children, and now your mind. The fact of the matter is that chemical imbalances are quite common in postpartum women. My mother's traumatic experiences triggered her mind to break down, bit by bit, with no explanation for the behaviors. Although I have a few fond memories of my mom, such as her as my class trip chaperone to the zoo and museum visits all throughout Philadelphia. Consequently, just like my mom, I too have traumatic memories too. While living in West Philadelphia as a child, the house was suddenly awakened by a loud crash coming from downstairs. It was in the wee hours of the morning; the sun had not even dawned yet. But I heard voices from downstairs, which sounded familiar. From the top of the stairs, I looked down, and there were my mothers' bloody hands. She had punched the living room window, and the shattered glass was everywhere. She began yelling and cursing, stating that her children were supposed to be with her. When the police arrived, I am sure they found themselves in an unusual situation, considering my father was a retired Philadelphia police officer with significant domestic issues. Although they were prepared to take her away due to trespassing, to ensure us kids were not being held against our will, the officers asked if I knew her and if I wanted to go home with her. In fear and without hesitation, I said no. I could not understand why she just didn't wait until we were awake to visit her. Then, she was escorted to the police car, and my mother was processed and booked for the disturbance. The unpredictable behavior she displayed led to us going to court, where the judge asked the same thing. "Who do you want to live with"? I knew normalcy came with my dad, and just like that, he was granted full custody. From that point on, my mom was determined to see her children by any means necessary. I mean, do you blame her? From that point on, we moved out of the city to the suburbs, about twenty minutes outside of Philadelphia, to Norristown. For a while, looking behind my back became a part of the norm. I quickly became numb to the hurt, embarrassment, and helplessness my motherless body could endure. Out of sight, out of mind was the prescription necessary to alleviate the damage. Since my dad worked as a teacher at the local high school, it was convenient for him to find babysitters easily. As such, some women became ready-made aunties. I guess this was the best option for me as a girl needing a feminine style to emulate. I may have been in the third grade when I was chaperoned by a young lady named Sandra, who had recently graduated high school and whose mom happened to be dating my dad. She took me under her wing and exposed me to the girly things most kids liked at that age. She did my hair and took me to places, but unfortunately, that was short-lived. We were headed to Center City one day to get my ears pierced. While walking hand in hand with Sandra towards the transportation center, I instantly saw my mom walking towards us. With a solid grip on Sandra's hand, my heart began racing, and I had no time to explain who this woman was to either party. I tried to hide my face nonchalantly before my mother recognized me. "Erika?" She spoke. I should've known she would do a double-take and realize it was me. She called my name once more, and this time, she tried to remove my hand from Sandra's. Quick-tempered, Sandra looked at me and questioned me; Do you know her?" I replied, "Yes, but I'm not supposed to go with her." Now, my mom was always "bout" it when it came to fighting. Before I knew it, my hand was ripped from Sandra's, and a fight between the two women immediately ensued. The newspaper stand fell over, and snacks were covered on the transportation center's floor, ruined. A few good men eventually broke the fight up, and we quickly made our way back home. I felt helpless as I retreated with the person who just beaten my mother's ass. That day has haunted me ever since. If only I could have helped her, encouraged her, or even hugged her. From that point on, my mom continued to battle her disability alone. As a child, I transferred to a different school every year until I was in the fourth grade. Switching schools so often impacted my learning capabilities, making it difficult to focus. My anxiety was at a level that no one knew existed. I didn't know when she'd show up, and when she did, there was always a dramatic scene. A memory that is sketched in my mind like a slow- motion picture. In fact, child development experts believe that children retain memories differently than adults. Meaning that children unpack memories that last a lifetime. According to Nora Newcombe, Ph.D., a psychology professor at Temple University, she says we all unpack memories into two distinct categories.

Explicit memory is associated with a time and a place. Whereas implicit memory is an emotional recollection. Consequently, some memories are not meant to be forgotten. It was a normal public-school day when an emergency developed. From what seemed like a simple fire drill at school, I was rushed out of the classroom to quickly discover that no other classmates were participating except me. Before I knew it, I was hiding underneath the principal's desk. My mother had just shown up, demanding to see her kids, she was escorted off the school premises. After this incident, during the following school year, my dad transferred us again to attend a private Catholic school. That transfer to St. Patrick's school was the best thing that happened to me. St. Pat's had an emphasis on a moral education, and it was the stability and acceptance I needed. My intent is never to vilify my family, but the truth about generational trauma is real. A portion of my mother's story will immensely shine a light on my own story. She was known as pretty Winnie, whose story is unlike any other. I plan to share her story in a future project, as I want to let the world know her story. I will always love my birth mother, "Winnie." She and my bonus mom indirectly helped me become the woman and mother I prayed to be. Someone who is nurturing, patient, a mentor, and a disciplinarian. Someone with the ability to give my children what I did not have. After ten years of my childhood without my mother, the day finally came for me to reunite with my mom. She was at her last home as a resident of a nursing facility in Ohio, totally disabled. I walked into her room, and there she was. My thoughts were that I'd finally gotten the opportunity to hear the truth. My mother-daughter conversation that I had longed for was finally upon me, but unfortunately, she was unable to speak. Her larynx was completely damaged. Although she needed assistance to stand up and hug me, she was determined and immediately blurted out my name, Erika! That moment was unforgettable.

It was as if her maternal instinct kicked in, and she knew the smell of her infant from nineteen years prior. Her illness had deteriorated the very things we take for granted every day. I am grateful for the time I spent with her. I painted her nails, we listened to music, and we had a connection. Radiating an air of tranquility that surrounded those around her, her face exuded serenity. The room was like a soothing calmness washed over the space, reminiscent of a gentle breeze on a warm summer day. A sense of calm filtered through the room. If she could talk, I would like to imagine that she was glad that her only girl made it through the chaos. I persevered through the uncertainties of life. Although leaving her in Ohio was difficult, living away from her was even more challenging. Living in a world of unanswered questions, she struggled to have an ordinary life. But so did I. A motherless child is no ordinary life either. The great emptiness is a tough space inside to fill. I sat in the front row at her funeral and didn't feel worthy enough to even occupy that space. I just wish I had done more for her when she was here. But what more could I have done? Those distressed thoughts circled my mind, but I left a piece of me right in her casket. My fourteen-karat gold cross necklace was strategically wrapped in her hands as she was laid to rest in preparation for her next home in glory. As a child without a mother, I am faced with a challenging reality. However, I refuse to use my circumstances as an excuse for anything. Rather than wearing an actual crown, I take pride in adorning the crown of persistence. It is a symbol of my unyielding power and relentless resolve. Although I cannot bring back my mother or even bonus mom, I think of them both often. Their names continue to play a melody on my tongue as I share their stories with my children and family, and even speak their names in spirit. I had to come to terms with my life being so different because I didn't have that mothering connection. I also realized that the individuals who enter your life do so with a specific intention and for a certain duration. I frequently reflect on the life I might have had with them and attempt to understand the purpose of their short-lived but profound influence on my life. That is because people only come into your life for a reason, and a season, or a lifetime. Meaning that we need to learn a lesson from them while they are in our lives. Most mothers advise their children to be ready for disappointment. Life is so full of unexpected events that you must be ready to handle setbacks and people who may disappoint you. The people who are in your life for a season are simply around us because we seek them to become better selves. However, there is a season of growth that takes place during which we are not needed any longer in that relationship. That said, I had to recognize that I don't need to be bitter, but rather appreciative. These are the people who may not have had your best interests in mind; they are the ones who may have insulted your intelligence or even demeaned you. But that's okay; I'm going to sit high on my throne as Beyonce sings, cause Mama says so. To all the moms out there who didn't have the love and support they needed from their own mothers, I want you to know that you are not alone. You didn't have the kind of mother who could fix a scraped knee or help you navigate the difficulties of growing up. Maybe she wasn't there for you on your wedding day or when you had your first child. But despite all of this, you have become a mother yourself. Sometimes, it can feel like an overwhelming task to lead your child down a path that was never shown to you. It's not easy to carry the weight of both the childhood you want to give your child and the childhood you never had. You might find yourself jealous at times of the amazing care your child receives, wishing that you had received the same love and attention when you were growing up. And there might be moments when you feel lost and uncertain about how to parent your child in the best possible way. But what you need to know is that you are always worthy of love. You deserved all the band-aids, Kleenex, and birthday dinners you never got. And if you didn't receive those things, it's not because of anything you did wrong. Maybe your mother never learned how to give love and support because she didn't receive it herself. Or maybe she was dealing with her own struggles and couldn't be there for you in the way you needed. The same sentiment applies to fathers as well. They, too, may have encountered their own difficulties and battles that prevented them from being there for their children. It's crucial to approach these situations with empathy and understanding, acknowledging that parents are human beings with their own baggage. By recognizing the potential reasons behind their shortcomings, we can start to heal and cultivate forgiveness. Remember, it is never about blaming or making excuses but about understanding the complexities of parental relationships but more about finding a path toward healing and growth.

CHAPTER 4

❦

IS BLOOD THICKER
THAN WATER?

"People raised on love see things differently than
those raised on survival." – Joy Marino

O f the six stepmothers I had; Mom Bee was the one who meant
the most to me. She was the one who left me through death
after six years. Too soon. Mom Bee was the most impactful in
my life, before and after her death. She was only thirty-eight years old when
she lost her life to cancer. my bonus mom - she was a force to be reckoned
with. For two years, I played the role of caregiver, bringing her meals,
tending to her gauze wraps, and talking about everything under the sun.
We connected on a deep level through our conversations, sharing our fears,
hopes, and dreams. It was during this time that I witnessed her fierce battle
with her illness, going through chemo, radiation, a mastectomy one
remission after another. But when she was well, her presence would light
up the room. Being around her was pure joy, as she brought laughter and

fun wherever she went. She truly was a remarkable woman, and I am forever grateful to have had her in my life. Her tall, slender stature and high-pitched voice was one of a kind. She was a true tomboy at heart, and that's a quality we both shared. Two individuals who could fearlessly run with the boys and effortlessly climb trees with a ray of beauty. Her inner beauty and adventurous spirit brought us closer together and created a unique bond that I cherished dearly. I could always count on her to join in on the fun and embrace life's adventures with enthusiasm. She showed me that being true to yourself, regardless of societal expectations, is a beautiful thing. I am forever grateful for the incredible memories we made together. She also inspired me to capture every photographic moment. Taking pictures was her thing, and I just adopted that same hobby. The real fact of the matter is that tomorrow isn't promised, so living in the moment is something I try to show and prove daily. Shortly after Mom Bee died, she came to me in spirit while I was sleeping in my room. Her mother, Grandma Ruby, was in the other room while I turned over to see her elbows and the glow of her face on the edge of my bed. As any human would do, I hysterically fell out of the bed and did a three-sixty on my feet until I fell to the floor. The chair on my desk ended up on top of me. She was gone, but that was my confirmation of her being all right. Grandma and I talked about it the next day over coffee, and she told me, "I knew it and heard it." We never spoke of it again. Mom Bee had the singing voice of an angel, a high alto that would have church members on their feet every time she sang a song. She even traveled all over the east coast, singing in choirs. I was about nine when she met my dad at the church, we all belonged to. She and her teenage son, who quickly became an adult and started his own family down south, leaving Mom Bee to quickly become a confidant and someone to look up to. I thought. Finally, another woman in my life and in my home and who can answer the questions about the facts-of-life that I had. When she talked to me, she didn't sugar coat anything. Her demeanor was stern and a matter of fact. She shared every black mom's word of advice that he could; from who to trust, not having kids, and how to recognize game. She constantly alerted me to superficial friendships and was a big advocate of fighting fair and square. Some people indeed come into your life for a reason and a season. She came into my life just in time to prepare this naïve little girl. I would like to think I got my shopping weakness from her. It was in the early nineties when we would spend our weekends hitting the mall. She drove a black Lincoln Town car with a burgundy interior. We connected on a level that was ordained by God, taking care of the basic needs that were neglected. She made sure I had clean and new panties and bras and supplied my maxi pads. My clothes were beautiful, and my hair was styled professionally as I was evolving into a young lady. On our shopping sprees, she would light up her cigarettes and blast her music, either gospel like Wilmington Chester Mass Choir or hits like "Be Thankful for What You Got by William DeVaughn, and that was me. I was thankful for a soul that took me under her wing to love me in a way that felt good. When I hear that song, I think of her. Everything has a message, and in hindsight, she taught me what I needed to know through this song. I must stand tall, even if I do not have the opportunities or materialistic things other people have. Sometimes, a song is all you need to get out of depression. She knew I had great potential and vowed to school me, even when it hurt me. Yes, those punches were brutal, especially when I was hardheaded and smart-mouthed, but that was only when I let my guard down. She had no idea I had already had such a tumultuous childhood. In other words, I had already built a pain tolerance, both emotionally and physically. Kinston, North Carolina, was home to Mom Bee, Grandma Ruby's daughter. During a family holiday gathering,

Mom Bee began reading my diary to the entire family. I quickly became the joke of the kitchen table as my writings revealed all my inner thoughts to everyone. Typically, one should never be surprised by what a teenage girl writes about. All I simply wrote about was having a crush on a boy, and that I had experienced bumping and grinding with that same boy. That same boy I was crushing on was an innocent moment, but we got to second base, and I revealed in my diary that I saw his pubic hair down there. Don't you know Mom Bee found my diary and read it to everyone. Unfortunately, my new family down south ridiculed and humiliated me based on my experience. From that point on, I began isolating myself to just my inner thoughts. I mean, I was a young girl coming into her own and discovering herself. Consequently, I could never escape that Cinderella feeling. I thought I knew Mom Bee loved me, but I didn't understand the level of humility she wanted me to learn. Although her family took me in as one of their own when I was a child, when I became an adult, I felt the blatant distinction that I was truly not family. Nevertheless, I persevered through betrayal, division and hurt. But I would go through that hurt a thousand more times to bring her back to life. The hurt from the loss of life is an empty and lonely feeling. Mom Bee's season in my life was cut short. I was robbed of what kind of felt like a normal life. Surely, there is no way God meant for me His child to go through this much abandonment. One month before my sixteenth birthday, she passed away at North Carolina Chapel Hill Hospital. Surrounded by her loved ones when she was taken off life support. It was a surreal moment, knowing I would never see her again. Just a year prior, we talked about her teaching me how to drive. Ironically, I ended up teaching myself how to drive when I would take my stepbrother's car. He had no idea that I took his car while he was playing at the basketball court. The thrill of getting away with it was awesome. I guess that's what sisters do. Nevertheless, Mom Bee's final wish to Grandma included the statement "Make sure y'all take care of Erika." Shortly after her death, Kinston became my newfound home. There was no way I was going to be able to live at liberty with just my dad, and me. So, I pleaded with my dad to move there. Grandma became my legal guardian, and from then on, her family embraced me and loved me as if I were born into the family. Grandma Ruby is truly an angel. Someone whose sole purpose is to love others while preaching the gospel of Jesus. Now that woman is strong! Three of her children predeceased her, and she is one of the strongest women I know, persevering past her own sorrows. It was a blessing in disguise that she was a part of my life. She represents the stability I have longed for all my life. People would even speak of the striking resemblances between my Aunt Della and me. That was Mom Bee's sister, just taller and more vulgar than Mom Bee. Full of love and laughter, Aunt Della took me under her wing. Since I was at a level of maturity most sixteen-year-olds were not at, I was able to explore adult vibes and nightlife scenes early. Although we were generations apart, I blended quite well with any crowd rolling with her, and it was guaranteed to be a good time. However, my curiosity about intimacy transitioned to a reality that quickly got out of control, using my promiscuity to drown myself in my own sorrows. I put myself in daring situations as if I had a beef with the kiss of death. While being careless with who I slept with. I began to cope with the abandonment by drinking and smoking cigarettes or marijuana. No matter what city I lived in, you could find me hanging out at a nightclub most weekends. In fact, I used Aunt Della's identification for years was used to gain entrance to quite a few clubs. Under the age of twenty-one, I had access to any club without anyone noticing the fifteen plus-year age difference between Aunt Della and me. Living on the edge was my motivation until one night a close friend of the family named Tiana and I went out of town to Rocky Mount, NC. We visited a guy I showed interest in and had been talking to by phone. When I arrived, things seemed great as we got to know each other over dinner. Afterwards, the plan was for him to invite some friends over to meet us. Everyone was having a good time as the music pumped and the drinks flowed. However, there was a point in time when my date and I spent some time in the bedroom while his friends continued to party in the living room with Tiana. Somehow, someway, someone must have slipped something into our drinks. I started getting extremely tired and needed to lie down on his bed. When I returned to my homegirl, she was surrounded by at least ten men in a circle with their pants down, waiting for their turn to penetrate. Unbeknownst to me, I could have been up next, but God's protection was on my side. My tolerance did not last long as I aggressively pushed several men off Tiana. They knew they were wrong and allowed us to leave as I helped her stand up and walk to the car. I had a figured at least two guys who had taken advantage of her and had sex with her. I also knew I was still under the influence of something, but I still proceeded to try and get us home. As I began to drive home under the influence, I was pulled over by a trooper. The trooper's first statement to me was that I was driving erratically. It was solely based on turning outside of the lines of the turning lane. He had no idea what we had just endured. Even though I had just saved my friend from getting gang raped. I know I would have gone to jail for DUI if I were required to get out of the car. So, I quickly straightened up, found a penny in my car's console, and hesitantly put it in my mouth. An old wise tale was that placing a penny under the tongue can disguise a breathalyzer. Thankfully, my wit and charm convinced the handsome officer that I was lost in the area, and he allowed me to proceed home. The reckless risks became serious enough to make changes. Therefore, I delved into what I knew most, which was my relationship with God. In solitude, I learned to listen to my heart and question why my path was so unusual. What was it about me that gave me a sense of protection regardless of the circumstances? How did I make it through the dangers and turmoil I came across? The lack of guidance and the limited mothering received became a plague on my life. I also questioned God, "Why me? I struggled with that consistent question all my life. However, I was bound to have this very testimonial moment. I've learned that some of the hardest times often lead to the greatest moments in life, and tough times are there to keep you going because they build strong people.

CHAPTER 5

⚬⚬

TRAUMATIZED

I survived because the fire inside me burned brighter
than the fire around me. – Joshua Graham

During the early 2000s, the late Aaliyah was undoubtedly one of my most cherished music artists. The mesmerizing tunes radiating from my trusty boombox often originated from her iconic track, 'Age Ain't Nothing but a Number'. While it holds some truth that age does not define maturity, it is undeniable that life experiences ultimately shape our level of growth. Aaliyah was a shining example of someone who had encountered and embraced experiences beyond her years and I felt the same way about myself. We both delved into realms that many individuals may only stumble upon much later in life, if at all. Seemingly, all my life, I have had to fight. Fight for love and opportunity, and on some occasions, fight for my life. I fought for love countless times. The first time I ever truly recognized fear was while fighting with someone I thought I loved. It just so happened to be with one of the most dangerous people I've ever known. He reminded me of "Nino Brown" from the old movie New

Jack City. He had the same occupation as Nino Brown. Once our relationship grew with time, I counted thousands of dollars, learned to cook, bag and weigh product. That was never a regular occurrence, but he made sure I knew some aspect of what was going on. Here I was subliminally living a lifestyle like the movie "Belly." We met while I worked as a cashier at the chicken spot, I was only seventeen. His eyes were dark and full of damage, something I was too familiar with. But we had a love that was intense, and I was down for all the goals and aspirations he had in mind. Consequently, the relationship became more abusive when we moved in together. He even bonded me out of jail when I had a conflict with my dad's ex-wife. I had no one else and he knew it. Our relationship grew toxic every day. His insecurities became imminent, as I could never be trusted. And to be honest, I wasn't trustworthy. The attention I desired was an afterthought to the empire he was building. We got to a point where we were fighting daily. One time, we fought in the middle of Queen Street, and thankfully, a friend of his saw the commotion from the barber shop, separated us, and calmed us down. Either of us could have gone to jail, considering we were right down the street from the police station. There were too many conflicts, and I knew I needed to leave the relationship. I just did not know how. My life depended on it, whether it was from fear of getting into legal trouble or fear of that last fight that would take my life. The last straw for me was during a fight at our duplex. I came in late and didn't expect him to be home. The streets usually had his attention, so my boyfriend staying home with me was rare. By the time I settled in and laid my head on the pillow. I was pulled out of the bed by my ankles. He had immediately accused me of being with another man. The truth is, I was another guy, but did I deserve the beating of my life? Before I knew it, I was in the fetal position as I was man-handled. This time, I had a black eye and visible bruises. He had never acted like this before. But he beat me so badly that I began screaming for help, hoping my neighbors would come to my rescue. Dragged from room to room by this man, I began to lose my dignity, and I was too beautiful for the bruises. The shame of my life had a stench, and I had to change it. So, shortly afterward, I planned for my escape. I left that man a few days after that last fight. He had no idea about my plans for an escape. And in the middle of the day, I left North Carolina. I headed back to Pennsylvania while he was at work. The only person who was aware of my plan was Grandma. I took nothing but a few trash bags full of clothes and my only television. That was all I needed where I was going. A fresh start in life was right before me. At last, I persevered out of that dark, abusive place in my life. A place of feeling invaluable, a place of fear. Once my dad got word of my abusive lifestyle, he got a hold of me and immediately began apologizing for turning his back on me. He was no longer with his wife and wanted to help me get back on my feet, return to school, and accomplish some goals. So, I drove back to my dad's place in a car with a bad transmission. My 'ninety-three electric blue Ford Taurus was so unreliable and my only way to my new beginning. I stopped for gas only once because I knew my vehicle would have the propensity to have me stranded on the highway. So, I drove non-stop until I couldn't any longer. But I desperately needed to fill up my gas tank to get me all the way home. Once I pulled over to a gas station in Delaware and headed back on the road, my transmission started slipping. I couldn't make it out of the parking lot, let alone back on I95. Immediately, I began to cry with my arms sheltering my face over the steering wheel. Here I was vulnerable, aggravated, and broken and all I could do was shout, "Why me?" It was as if God had left me hanging even when I was trying to get my life together. My spirit just couldn't take any more disappointments. After my emotional breakdown,

I put the car in drive, and just like before, my transmission started skipping' again. Then suddenly, a burst of power funneled through, and I was back rolling up north. If you've ever had transmission problems, you could understand my level of anxiety while driving. In any event, I made it on a wing and a prayer. And that prayer was heard loud and clear as angels guided my way home. That was just the encouragement I needed where I was going. When I finally got to Norristown, my dad helped me get back on my feet for a year until he moved back south. I was able to secure a job, create a social life, and give myself a shot at relationships again. I was proud of myself. I was proud of the woman I was becoming, especially after leaving Kinston in such an emotional state of mind and overcoming such a dark moment in my life; it was a win. I was mesmerized by danger, and that is what made me scared for my life. But at just twenty years old, focused on my fresh start. I quickly enrolled at the local college and began working full-time as a residential counselor for a mental facility. Thankfully, my responsibilities of working and paying bills came easy for me. It was second nature, and Ms. Independent was a tune to which I could highly relate. And nine times out of ten, you would find me on the dance floor to Neo's song, which in my mind, was made especially for me. I was determined to somehow buss a groove in this life, which was why I lived so freely. A wise person once told me that abusive men don't lose control; they only lash out when they can't gain the control they're looking for. The movie "The Color Purple" by Alice Walker, has always connected to my emotional state ever since I was a child. This was one of the first movies I connected with, with all the subliminal elements. Specifically, Celie's children who were raised in Africa without her. From childhood to adulthood, I remembered the lines from each scene almost verbatim. Especially the infamous quote, "All my life I had to fight." I said that often and attributed it to my internal struggles.

This time, I thought I hit the jackpot by dating a man who was an on-air TV personality for a local hip-hop show. One night, I went to visit a friend who was the bartender at a bar on South Street in Philadelphia. They held karaoke on Wednesday nights, and it just so happened that the hip-hop TV show was there. Honestly, I had no idea who he was. I simply did not watch the show because it aired in the wee hours of the morning. I was either sleeping or out in the night scene. However, the on-air personality quickly became my love interest. He was flamboyant and would light up a room as he carried his photo album, featuring pictures of him with music artists and actors on many occasions. This album would have hundreds of pictures of him posing with celebs, including one of him with Biggie Smalls, one of the greatest rappers of all time. Although my new man was much shorter than what I was used to; that did not stop his desire for taller women. He was creative as hell, known in the hip-hop industry, and his enthusiasm for his craft was like nothing I had seen before, and it could have led him to higher heights. And I was here for it. Eventually, he began to mentor me, and I received firsthand experience at a few on-air opportunities. From outtakes to commercials and cross-promotions, this man gave me access to something I had never experienced. During major events in the city, we had free entry thanks to his press badge, so at any given time, A-list celebrities surrounded me. Musiq Soulchild was one of my favorite artists at the time. Especially when he dedicated a snippet of his song to me during an interview. I was on top of the world, and our relationship quickly evolved into a living-together situation. Instead of us staying in West Oak Lane, where he previously lived, and he didn't want to go back home to Germantown, he moved in with me to Norristown. We met each other's families and were on the fast lane to marriage when we were engaged one year into our relationship. But unfortunately, I was blindsided by his dreams versus reality. Not only did he lie about his age, claiming to be five or six years my senior, when he was really twelve years older than me. I found out more truths after we lived together, making our relationship a false report. Eventually, contracts became shortlisted at the show, and the local production studio was sold, therefore making his income limited to a car washer at a dealership. The stress and devalued man rapidly changed. And as a result, he became violent. We had just left the store and began to argue about something trivial. As we got into the car, he proceeded to get into the back seat. I did not think anything of it, but I continued to plead my case. Meanwhile, my attitude shifted, and I know I said some vulgar things, but that's just how I roll. During this, I was sucker punched in the face from the back seat. I quickly pulled over to cry. I couldn't drive but mustered up the strength just to get home. That was the end of our relationship, engagement, and cohabitation. The triggering behavior of physical violence is something that has plagued me. I refused to be a statistic and hurtfully let him go. I am an advocate of domestic violence. People can disagree without physical violence. Besides, I am no good to anyone from six feet below. Have you ever experienced something so traumatic that you started analyzing your purpose in life? In 1985, I lived in West Philadelphia in a row home with my dad and brother. Although I was young, it wasn't unusual to find us kids playing outside without supervision. One summer day, I was following my brother and the other neighborhood kids when suddenly, I was hit by a vehicle that resembled the car from the "Dukes of Hazard" show. Even though I spotted the car at the beginning of the block, my timing was off, and I was too young to make that determination. I thought I could make it but ended up being hit head on by the car. In those days, if a person could brush it off, they didn't have to go to the hospital, and the driver was never charged for the accident. Although I suffered a nosebleed and a concussion, it was a frightening experience. What was even more traumatic was that, after being hit by the car, it was as if I had awakened before I stood up. That moment has been affixed to my mind all my life. God Almighty was gracious enough to give me another chance, a chance to see a tomorrow, and gracious enough to send His angels to watch over me, especially when life's stressors and situations were impacted by an unforeseen chain of events. I was only nineteen and traumatized when Tiana and I were on our way to choir rehearsal. We were already running late, but as she drove with expediency, we were suddenly stopped at a standstill. In front of us, we saw three to five cars that had already stopped. But what we were not expecting was a low-flying object just standing in the sky. It was only about fifty yards up, sitting at a standstill. There were no propellers, and the circular-shaped object had lights around it and was certainly on another level of brightness. We were both in amazement at what we were looking at. Quickly, Tiana made our left turn, and before we knew it, the UFO turned left and started following us. Upon noticing, I was straight-up scared! Crying and praying all at the same time. The smooth, cylinder-like stealth glided through the trees parallel to the road we were driving on. Afraid for my life, the thought of abduction was real for me, and I'm thankful I didn't have to experience this alone. Within another 30 seconds of that tormenting moment, the UFO completely disappeared. Finally, Tiana and I arrived at choir rehearsal, panicked by what we had just experienced. We ran inside the church and told our story to the group. Folks looked at us like we were crazy or on drugs. For years, I rarely spoke of it, but now it's not unusual for people to have had similar experiences and I felt compelled to share mine. The Epitome of Perseverance is all about a testimony. A verification of the hardships I experienced, which could have and should have held me back, but instead,

I made something out of nothing. With no regrets and always in the moment because life as we know it can flash before our very eyes and I'm a living witness to that. It was a typical summer afternoon, and I was twenty-one years old, arriving home from work. The clouds were dark on one side of the street with lightning; in contrast, they were sunny on the other. As I began to take coverage towards my home, I stepped on the first step of my home. Suddenly, a bolt of lightning hit a power line, and that same power line hit the fourth step. To comprehend, the capacity of electrical voltage from power lines is typically between 4,800 and 13,200 volts. In comparison, the voltage typically used with electric chairs is between 5,000 and 200 volts. If I'd arrived two seconds earlier, I would have been electrocuted. Just imagine my reaction when it all happened. In slow motion, it appeared as if I knew taekwondo with the moves I made trying to retreat in three-inch heels. Unfortunately, that resulted in a twisted ankle, but with a grateful heart. To clarify, my job was something I took immense pride in. I was willing to make a career out of it, as I studied Psychology at West Chester University. As a residential counselor on the grounds of Norristown State Hospital, building fifteen was a place that taught me, terrified me, and loved me all at the same time. When I was originally hired there, I worked the third shift from eleven to seven. Six months later, I was hired for a full-time position from three to eleven in the evening, which was the most active shift. And we all agreed! In fact, during shift change, my colleagues would remind us to always "expect the unexpected." That infamous quote guided my day-to-day life as there was never a dull moment with the responsibility of twenty-four residents with mental health issues. Twelve men and twelve women; I took on six in my caseload, and this facility was a positive step toward living independently. Little did they know, this place also took me on a journey of independence.

This was one of the first solid jobs I held since leaving North Carolina. Not only did I have an advancement opportunity as the youngest with supervisory duties, but I also volunteered in the mental health community. I'd like to think that my unique childhood was relatable enough for me to compare it with their mental struggles. Although I wasn't the person for everyone, there was a connection to many. However, one day, my manager called me at home before my shift to warn me that a resident was on a rampage. She threatened to cut my throat, and her intimidation was not taken lightly. When I arrived at work, the police were there to escort me through the side door while escorting her out the front. After years of mental anguish, I started to become immune to the characteristics that made people snap; still, there were certain triggers that could send even me over the edge. That's why it's important to care for the caregiver while giving them the time needed to regroup their thoughts and emotions. Simply because the impact of traumatic events can cause a person to either handle them negatively or positively. And with all the effort I had in my being, I needed to stay positive. And although I was practicing what I was going to school for, majoring in Psychology. However, I felt the desire for change leading up to the hostage situation that occurred. Working as a residential counselor, I truly made an impact on the work I was doing and the lives that I helped. But I was already broken, bandaged and way too young to subject myself to even more crises. Unfortunately, a woman lost her life, and that was the crucial moment I knew I needed a change for my own mental sake. But I had to endure another traumatic experience first. It was the spring of 1999, and I worked directly across the street from where a former worker or client came back to retaliate after losing his job. It was a two-day hostage standoff on the hospital grounds, and I continued to work my shift. While the SWAT team negotiated with the shooter, the residents, my colleagues, and I were re-located in another part of the campus. However, the community speculated that law enforcement and SWAT could have managed this emergency differently. Who knows? A life could have been saved. Thankfully, my building was not directly involved and considered just a bystander but working through the chaos seemed like the longest three days of my life. SWAT negotiations did not go well and began to agitate the shooter. Eventually, the shooter became even more irritated, and he shot and injured one woman and then killed another woman. Immediately, a sniper took him out and killed him. You see, these traumatic experiences have all changed my life in some way. And as a traumatized child, I always thought someone would come and save me from all my ordeals. But what I didn't expect was that someone to be me. After healing from trauma, I created a new mindset. A mindset of strength, joy, courage, and wisdom. And I am personally proud of my perseverance as a survivor.

CHAPTER 6

❦

ALWAYS JUDGED BY THE COVER

"Sometimes, I feel discriminated against, but it does not make me angry. It merely astonishes me. How can any deny themselves the pleasure of my company? It's beyond me."
– Zora Neale Hurston

N ever judge a book by its cover," a widely recognized quote, but how often do we actually adhere to it? It may appear cliché, but I have consistently suffered from being unfairly stigmatized due to others' lack of effort. I am a complex individual who requires sincere dedication to truly understand." Although I don't look like what I have been through, people tend to treat me like an afterthought. If it were me not having children until I was thirty-four, then most would believe something was wrong with me. Or how about the fact that I was born with a resting bitch face? Most people think I'm sad or mad when they first meet me. My husky voice can be intimidating or even over- sexualized, and it all depends on how you read me. My skillset has mostly been based on life experiences. I wanted to match those life experiences with the intellectual prowess I knew I had deep within me. Insinuating that my intelligence was not up to par seemed far too easy for others to judge. I just never tried to prove anyone wrong; instead, I did the work and just succeeded. As a newcomer at my former high school, I was met with this same judgment. What started as a convenience ended up as a challenge, and this was mainly due to transferring too many credits. Nevertheless, it was well worth my while to consider graduating early. Especially since my dad no longer needed to pay tuition at my old private school from when we lived up north. But when I relocated back down south, it was a different story. The guidance counselor, Ms. Dickson, at Kinston High had other plans for my future. After initially approving me for early graduation, she later backed out of that approval. This was only due to another student complaining that she wasn't given that opportunity. My grades were sufficient, and I had ordered regalia and even made graduation plans, including attending the class trip to the Bahamas. However, Ms. Dickson took it upon herself and made an extreme decision based on emotions. There was no just cause for her holding me back four months before graduation other than her thinking she was being fair. My dad had no leverage as he would have up North, and my legal guardian didn't know how to fight this battle for me. The impact of this decision could have been cataclysmic for my future. I later found out that the excuse that was eventually given to me by Ms. Dickson was fraudulent. There are no NC laws that say you must have four years of English. In fact, students continue to use this method throughout the state. This would have forced me to stay another year at the high school only to take electives and the one English class I needed. And to make matters worse, all my peers assumed that I was held back; to this day, many still believe that. So, as an alternative, I decided to take my remaining courses at the local community college, which allowed me to graduate that same year at sixteen years old. Besides, I was already accustomed to independent living, and returning to high school for another year was just not beneficial for me at the time. What Ms. Dickson did not realize was that I was one of a kind, and that the path I was destined to take was not supposed to be average. One of the most impactful men of our time, Rev. Dr. Martin Luther King Jr., once said, "Don't allow anybody to make you feel that you are a nobody, always feel that you count, always feel that you have worth, and always feel that your life has ultimate significance." This should be the blueprint for all black children. I just wish I had this affirmation in my ear when I was a child because I have always been judged by the cover. Eventually, I proudly completed my Bachelor of Science degree in management with a Professional Project Management certificate. Ten years later, I completed a major milestone by earning an MBA. It was a personal victory that validated my self-worth and I demonstrated that no one could undermine my potential. The journey to obtaining my degree filled my heart with so many emotions, sweat and tears, but I remained resolute in my determination to succeed. Despite the challenges, I refused to let anything hold me back and returned to the classroom just three weeks after giving birth to my second child, a testament to my unique perseverance. I am naturally motivated towards multitasking due to my inherent strength; the strength I needed to withstand the judgement. So, I decided to just let people misunderstand and judge me. Judging a book by its cover means that you can't characterize someone's value by just their outside appearance. But what I will not allow is for someone to sit high and look low to judge me because what they can't see on the outside is the journey I traveled to get where I am. Everyone has a story and has been through some kind of turmoil that has changed them. It's unfair to form opinions about someone based on a single encounter. I have experienced this misconception from various people, whether they are former colleagues or acquaintances from church. I'm a multifaceted individual who requires time and effort to truly understand. Appearances can be deceiving and do not reveal much about a person's true character or experiences. Unfortunately, it's easy for people to jump to conclusions, but I try to avoid being hypocritical myself. It's surprising how much pain people can conceal behind a cheerful facade, often stemming from unspoken trauma and struggles. Sometimes, these hidden scars can cause toxicity in friendships and with family, but confronting these issues is necessary for healing. Despite my outward strength as a black woman, I'm not immune to emotions. While I may seem a bit rough around the edges and display a mix of bougie and ghetto qualities, I remain fiercely loyal to those close to me. Loyalty means so much to me, but you can't force it. And I find myself wondering why loyalty to me isn't reciprocated. Support coincides with loyalty because it exposes consistency. A social media influencer, Trent Shelton, once said, "Life has taught me that you can't control someone's loyalty." "No matter how good you are to them, doesn't mean they'll treat you the same". "No matter how much they meant to you, doesn't mean they'll value the same." Sometimes the people you love the most, turn out to be the people you can trust the least." Growing up in a household dominated by males, my brother tended to bully me. It could have stemmed from the lack of motherly care. However, I also believe that he was the favorite child which may have contributed to his lack of compassion. During our childhood, he frequently insulted my intelligence, making it seem like I had no hope of succeeding. My father seemed to enjoy the joke, fueling my brother's teasing. Perhaps their goal was to tear me down and discourage me from pursuing my goals. Despite the many challenges I faced, I refused to give up or let anyone stand in the way of my success. As one of the greatest, Bob Marley, once said, "Who are you to judge the life I live? I know I'm not perfect, and I don't live to be. But before you start pointing fingers, make sure your hands are clean." I was only sixteen years old when my best friend confided in me and told me that she was raped by her father. I thought it was kind of weird when I witnessed him slapping her on the butt when she was washing her hair in the kitchen sink. It made me cringe, and I was certainly glad that my dad wasn't that close to me like her father. However, she was my blood sister, and I vowed that I would not tell anyone. And when I say blood sister, it was based on cutting our fingers and mingling them with each other. This was an old school confirmation of friendship. Meaning that we were just that important to each other. That was until I couldn't hold that secret of her being rapped any longer. I tussled, withholding that information for too long as I was concerned for her. Eventually, I told my grandmother, with the hope that she would get my sister some help. Maybe he would be interrogated by someone so that he could see the error in his ways. But that's not how it turned out. Once my grandmother told her pastor, and all parties were informed of the rape. Nothing happened. Instead, I was ridiculed as being an out-of-control kid with no parental control. I was no longer permitted a friendship with my blood sister, and I was judged instead of believed. I was perceived as the one who was up to no good and would never amount to anything. That was so disheartening, and I'll never forget the look of ignorance from adults when my sister girl ended up pregnant. I knew it was not her boyfriend from high school, but at that point, my tongue had already said enough. My reputation was damaged from telling the truth, and I learned to stand still and live in the midst of judgment.

Living in judgment isn't for everyone. It takes a level of resilience that comes from inner strength. The strength it takes to rebound when you face a loss, a setback, or a challenge. Although adversity doesn't go away, people will always judge the book by the cover. And it took resilience to protect my peace and mental health and just move on. Knowing that when people count you out, God counts you in because difficult paths can lead to beautiful destinations.

CHAPTER 7

❧

THE ROSE THAT GREW FROM CONCRETE

"Do not judge me by my successes, judge me by how many times I fell down and got back up again."
– Nelson Mandela

It is almost impossible for a rose to thrive in an uncomfortable place like the middle of concrete. The foundational roots have a limited environment due to the weight of the concrete, yet they still have the propensity to grow. Unfortunately, over time, the alkaline in the concrete will deprive the roots of necessary nutrients, but they can blossom. The rose is one of the most aromatic plants and is known to some botanists as the queen. Coincidently, it is symbolic of peace and love all around the world. There was so much significance in ancient times to the dynamics of the rose. Queens were known to use roses in incense, aphrodisiacs, garlands, perfumes, wines, and food. In addition, Jews, Christians, and Muslims all viewed the rose as a symbol of love. In fact, the history of the Greeks used to associate a five-petaled rose as a symbol of Aphrodite, the goddess of love and beauty. In the sixth century, Christianity associated red roses with a celebration of martyrs who reached heaven or the afterlife. Historical records from the sixth century even reference the "Day of the Roses," I can imagine one's funeral in those times being filled with an array of roses. However, the Holy Bible references thorns more often than roses. I'd like to think that the pain from the thorn symbolizes lessons to be learned from the darkest days in life. In the book of Song of Solomon, it's interpreted that the female compares herself to the Sharon of rose, and in another stanza, she compares herself to a rose among thorns. Sometimes, I feel as if I am the only rose in a room of thorns, otherwise known as haters. However, God uses difficult situations to not only humble you but also to teach you to depend on His grace alone; only under such circumstances will this only by that rose in the room rise. To show up and be victorious regardless of who is against me. Just as the Jews were against Jesus, not only did they make a mockery of Him, but they also tried to hurt Him and break His spirit with the crown of thorns pressed into his head. But soon after, HE persevered to see His purpose through; after a while, the pain wasn't even a factor. So, when I'm ridiculed, ostracized, and talked about behind my back, I visualize how unbothered Jesus was and try to emulate the same sentiment. I use the thorns as a defense mechanism for those who don't treat me right, and in turn, I laugh, smile, and keep it moving. People are limited in the grace they give to others, and that's okay because I'd rather be receive grace only from God. Without sounding holier than thou, God can use an imperfect soul just like mine. Just to show where my source of perseverance comes from. My past is full of tough circumstances, and I solely depend on God's grace to see me through my triumph. Not focusing on the physical pains resulting from depression, anxiety, illnesses, disabilities, or even unfulfilled desires, but enduring to the very end. The rose that grew from concrete is so profound because it recognizes one's imperfections. How you see yourself is more important than how others see you. The words you speak and affirm have greater consequences because you choose to believe them. I had to understand that my past mistakes didn't make me less worthy of love, goodness, kindness, success, and everything I prayed for. I was deserving of every good thing. While firmly believing in my purpose against all odds, this is what makes the journey even more special, confirming that I am royalty along this path called life. The poem "The Rose that grew from Concrete," written by the late great Tupac Shakur, is encouraging and appears to characterize some of my life's journey. The poem is not actually talking about the rose flower and the concrete. The rose symbolizes an individual, while the concrete stands for the ghetto. There's no way a rose flower would grow from concrete. Meaning that it's very hard for someone to survive the hard life of the ghetto and be successful. Yet, a person can still survive if they're ready to swim against nature's law. Nature's law says that no one is expected to survive life in the ghetto. But that can be proven wrong if they can push through life. That's what I have been inspired to do. Every time an opportunity was taken, or I was disappointed, I still had goals. Keeping those dreams and goals alive is what makes you a survivor of the harsh realities of life. Tupac felt that people should be confident in their abilities to reach goals. If one continues to persevere, they can get to a place far away from the ghetto and never face problems anymore. At that point, one will be able to achieve one's goals and aspirations. Tupac's timeless, poetic rhymes are respectable truths that empowered me to focus on my dream and making them a realization. Not dwelling on the circumstances that have held me back could no longer be an excuse.

CHAPTER 8

❦

EVERYTHING HAPPENS FOR A REASON

*What seems to us as bitter trials are often
blessings in disguise – Oscar Wilde*

My life changed dramatically when I met the love of my life. This man became my concrete, and I his rose as he held me down with the love and attention I had always longed for. I had already had my fair share of frogs to kiss to get my prince, so it was well worth the wait. I took a chance on love when we met in 2009 by way of us both being participants in someone's wedding. In fact, our story is truly one of a kind, a match made from heaven. I was a thirty-year-old socialite when my former apartment neighbor asked me to not just attend her wedding, but also be a bridesmaid. She even provided the dress. It was the month of October as I walked down the aisle of a man-made brick staircase. Ironically, I walked past my future husband as I took my bridesmaid spot. What made this relationship so inspirational? I was honest and vulnerable while I explained to him that I had been looking for love in all the wrong places. That's when I let him know that I was already in a dead-end relationship with someone else, and coincidently, so was he. That was the commonality that brought us together, we both had dates who decided not to attend the wedding since they were Caucasian. Our "should-have-been dates" gave the same excuse as to why they didn't want to attend the wedding with us. Sounds selfish, right? This was by no coincidence; it was divinely ordered for us. After our friend's wedding, we talked on the phone for eight hours straight that night. The next day, he invited me to his church. It was a small grassroots church, which was something I was accustomed to, considering my father was a former pastor. Although the circumstances surrounding our initial courtship outweighed any couple's success, we defied the odds. When we met, my husband had already had two failed marriages, two children by two different women, and their other kids, whom he loved as well. He had no job and had just moved into a home with his mother and five-year-old son at the time. There is no way I would have given this man a shot, considering all the odds not only stacked against him but also against us as a couple. The beauty in this story is that the rose metaphorically represents our marriage, and the concrete represents the obstacles. The petals of a rose can wither, fade, dry out, and fall off. But with the right love, communication, respect, and the perseverance to make it work. Because every relationship can go into a season of disappointment. The challenge is recognizing when your marriage is going through a difficult time. Because in 2012, before family and friends, we sealed the deal. I promised to love him, and he vowed to me that this marriage would persevere in good times and in bad. It's just easier to hope for a smooth experience. Within the first year of our marriage, we embarked on a spiritual journey together, with him as a youth pastor and me working in ministry as a Sunday school teacher, youth choir director, and choir member. However, my husband's calling seemed more pertinent. We lived everything for the ministry of the church, so much so that it wasn't long before I resented that his obligation to the church cost him less time to be with his family. I thought I was on a love journey with this man and surely, God didn't call my husband to abandon his newly formed family. I was bitter that I was raising our children alone. And as a result, my husband's commitment to me seemed no longer a priority to me. Out of seven days a week, it wasn't usual for him to be mandated there for at least five days. Not to mention, he worked a full-time job for eight to ten hours a day. My spirit was weakening, and this subliminal rose began to wither. And to make matters worse, people began to try me. Newly married and in a new church, along with my first experience as a mother took a toll on me. Not only did I not have a mother to share this moment with, but I didn't have much help either. "And, despite the unique mental impact of postpartum, individuals often challenge your resilience, causing you to be unfairly labeled as the troublemaker or unapproachable. To promote fairness, it becomes incredibly important to question the presence of double standards and evaluate them based on spirituality instead of solely relying on religion. Cause this girl got a spirit of discernment. But it's disheartening how swiftly people point out your behavior in specific situations yet fail to recognize their own wrongdoings." I can recall being at church one Sunday and someone attempted to kidnap my child. My baby was in the carrier on the floor near me and while I was focused on someone else, the woman grabbed the car seat carrier and went out of the door. She had already made it halfway to her car before I realized it. The church member took the carrier and thought it was a joke after I ran after her to get my baby. It took months before I would even speak to her. As Christians, we're expected to turn the other cheek, but the trust was already broken, and I was still working on avoiding conflict. We eventually made peace, but I started noticing a heavy weight on my shoulders. And unexpectedly, I began to have my guard up and feeling defensive when I stepped foot in the church. The musician chastised me for missing a certain Sunday when I took a weekend to do a wellness check on my father. Soon after I returned, the musician called me into his office and asked me to have a seat. Immediately, I was overcome with discernment and felt that I was going to need to be on defense. He got right to the point and abruptly asked, "What's more important, family or ministry?" I thought to myself, after all the time and energy my family and I has sacrificed to be there, this man wants to check me on missing a Sunday?" I abruptly got up from my seat and rolled my neck with a fierce attitude, and in astoundment, I shouted, "Family!" Just as Jesus turned the tables in the temple, I let it be known that God didn't intend to separate family. I quickly made a scene in the hallway with the pastor and other minister present. Although I had genuine intentions, I was scorned for my delivery. Subsequently, I wore the badge of scorn with pride because I rebelled against something deep down, I still believe was wrong. But my courage to stand up for myself in spite of led to the pastor removing me from my position. I was the director for more than fifty children from ages five to eighteen. And when I tell you the impact of children doing something positive was significant, believe me. Sure, I could have handled my reaction better, but I had already felt that I was an intended target. I should have been prepared for the change because I had already grown accustomed to people that I loved to abandon me. However, I found myself with a newfound freedom, and less commitment, but my husband's commitment never changed. Leaving us even farther apart. But the Lord stood with me and gave me strength. I came to terms with our lives being officially separated by worship. However, I knew our purpose as a union was much greater and something had to change. What did I do? I prayed for change. It wasn't unusual for me to convene with just me and God alone. I was vulnerable and I prayed for another life. I prayed for and wanted my marriage to be unified, not divided. He can certainly love God and still help raise our kids, right? I began to realize that people's interpretations of what the church should look like aren't the end-all-be-all. God has nothing to do with the hurt experienced in the church. He is a sovereign God, and I recognized that the issues and disappointments I was experiencing were just a test, and I didn't feel confident in my evaluations. I started noticing that our marriage wasn't being nurtured, and the man that I fell in love with was changing. Sure, he was tired; he seemed to spread himself too thin, and I was suffering for it. And just like that, the world stopped. I have always said, "the 2020 pandemic was a blessing and a curse." Not only did I have my husband back at home and in tune with what was happening at home, but it also brought us closer in our marriage and our relationship with God. Too many times, do we worry about how men treat us? The reality is that some people are mad because you aren't suffering the way they expected you to. Whether it's friends, family, or foes, I realized that my help comes from God, and I don't have to deal with anything or anyone that doesn't bring me peace. Besides, God is love, and if people were to tap into a godlier spirit; the harm done by other people wouldn't even be a factor. In fact, the more healing that I have done, the more comfortable I am with knowing that I might be perceived as the villain in the story by people who don't want to heal themselves.

CHAPTER 9

❧

CYCLE BREAKERS

*Today, the toxicity stops with me. I deserve to be loved in a
way that shows compassion, comfort, and trust. Let your
truth break the cycle of generational curses and live
the life you aspire to. – Erika Rose Paige*

A cycle breaker is someone who recognizes the harmful dysfunctional traits that exist in the culture of the family. The cycle breaker has the power to change those family habits that cause such pain and grief. Childhood trauma has damaged so many people; it affects your sense of self, and then you waste time trying to figure out the reason for parents' failures. No person should feel alone, ignored, or isolated due to trauma. Living as a motherless child, most days, I felt alone. And although my father was present and loved me the best way he could, there were times that I felt like I didn't matter. But I knew I mattered, and I knew that perception had to change. I wanted my family and friends to love me the way I wanted to be loved, with no limitations. And to do that, it started with me breaking the cycle and recovering from the hurt of past behaviors. You can't recover until you know what you're recovering from. Generational curses are bad habits or behaviors that are passed from one generation to the next. Although parents strive to ensure they lead a life that will help their children live a better one, the future of any child depends greatly on the family they come from. This is because we learn patterns and values and form opinions about ourselves and things from the people we spend most of our time with. If a child grows up in a wild hood, there is a tendency for that child to turn out to be a wildling in the future. I guess that's what my dad was trying to prevent when he moved us out of the city and into the burbs. Although children practice what they have learned on their own and what they have gathered from generations before them, this is not automatically a terrible thing because the lessons you were taught when you were younger can be a guide for you later in life. If you want to see the trajectory of where your family will end up, looking back often paints a clear picture. Many times, people attribute generational curses to demons, and. maybe they were right about it. However, I understand generational curses as bad decisions and wrong family patterns that have been passed from one generation to another. As a young adult, I had so much freedom to make and drown myself in all the wrong choices, but God saw me through. Where there was no love and warmth, He was always there in the depths of the meaningless darkness. Living in a one-parent home is a generational cycle that has plagued many families, including mine. And although I had my bonus mom to share with for a short period of time, I processed my emotions all by myself. If you can imagine how traumatic life had been for me before the legal age of eighteen, I had the pain of being second fiddle to my brother and not feeling valued enough. That, combined with the challenges of adult life, can make it difficult to live a quality life. But giving up isn't an option, so start bending those ugly generational patterns. Without my faith, I would never have had the courage to become the rose that grew from concrete. That is an unusual story and unusual testimony. As a result, I aim to live a life of purpose, that has value, full of love, yet not naïve to ulterior motives. However, I had to ask myself if I could really break cycles and open-up without the fear of failure, rejection, and heartache. I even analyzed my history of over giving in relationships, making unhealthy choices, and finding out who the real Erika was. In a nutshell, it's all about ups and downs, strengths and weaknesses, and the joys and sorrows of life. And during this process, I've realized that it's hard to trust since my feelings change like the seasons. I would tend to shield my heart with an armored defense, especially when I am ridiculed, and that is accompanied by stench of attitude. The truth is, there is no protection from the ignorance of others due to an uncommon life. But once I discovered my purpose and pursued it vigorously. I knew that another critical part of my journey was breaking generational curses. Healing was a journey, an unending one. It is unending because, down the road, you'd still stumble on a page of hurt that wasn't previously opened, but it is okay. You can take as long as possible to find your healing but never get drowned in there. I needed to be completely honest with myself to embark on the journey of total healing. I had to acknowledge that something was wrong with my family and be courageous enough to address it. I had already come this far and couldn't back down. Hurt is tricky; it can hide in the deepest recesses of your soul, waiting to show its ugly face in the event of your success. I was smart enough to understand that some celebrities who got hooked on drugs and liquor had only been using them to cover up their pain. Pain is a powerful force that, if left unresolved, can impact future generations. My parents' love, although filled with good intentions, inadvertently carried their own unresolved pain that affected me deeply. It had been a union of two broken people whose hearts were crying out for authenticity and comfort. My father, a deeply devout man had an unwavering devotion to God. Despite his strong faith there were parts of him that remained broken. While he loves me, his unresolved pain would sometimes manifest as emotional distance or overprotectiveness. My mother carried her own share of pain, but the origins of her brokenness started in childhood. Perhaps it was the heartache of being separated from her children, or maybe it was the profound loss of the love of her life. Additionally, the pressure from family members seemed to contribute to her internal struggles. Whatever the cause, her pain seeped into the fabric of our family. These are honest reflections. One night, I woke up and grabbed myself a cup of coffee. I can't tell why I had that craving; perhaps my body was telling me I needed a little boost for what I had prepared myself to do. After downing the warm cup of bittersweet liquid, I stood before my dressing mirror and gave a good look at the woman in the reflection. There was raw pain in her eyes and a plethora of invisible scars on her body. This was my moment, and I was the only one who could truly see myself and truly understand the phases of pain that I had gone through. Healing was personal, and I had the power in my hands. A pool of hot tears burned my eyes as painful memories flooded my mind. Still, I had to be strong and ask the necessary questions. How have the patterns in my family affected me? Was I willing to pass this on to my children? I sobbed as I imagined my future babies going through every layer of pain that had washed over me. When I couldn't imagine such a life of emotional torture, lies, rejection, and pain, I made up my mind to end the ugly patterns of my parents with me. My father had a little problem with married life. And although he's a good man, there wasn't much stability in his love life. My biological mother had been plagued with a disease that could've been genetic enough to have been passed on to me, but it wasn't. The pattern here was being a child in a single-parent home. I was the offspring of two companions who were once in love; I was a descendant of lost love. And if I hadn't been careful, and with the guidance of the Holy One, who chose to spare my life and give it a purpose, I would've given up a long time ago. Overwhelmed by the dark voices inside my head. "It all ends right now. It ends here, Erika." My lips had silently moved as I stared at the woman in the mirror. But breaking generational patterns that were ugly wasn't just talk. I knew it would take hard work. I had to consciously renounce my parents' decisions and what they caused me. I had to humble myself to reach out to the deepest gap in my soul and exhume every trauma hidden there. I bared it all out. You can't get healed when you're covered up. You must acknowledge the curses and problems, size them up, and consciously renounce them. I had to value myself and walk with the right crowd, too. I also prayed to be blessed with a gorgeous king who could understand the need for pure love and warmth. I wanted my children to thrive in healthy places; this would be evidence that such curses had been broken. King David created a generational curse by committing adultery. He had a flaw in womanizing, and that solidified a foundation for his future sons. When Solomon became king, not only did he push forward the generational curse, but he also loved women from forbidden cultures. That story always did something inside of me. I saw generational curses as seeds. The more a bloodline progressed, the stronger the tree of this curse grew until one person was conscious enough to stand against it. In my case, I had taken a stand on the decision to end single- parent families. I had to take a stand against physical and verbal abuse of children. I had taken a stand against invalidating the emotions of children, bullying them to submission, and saying hurtful words that could damage their self-esteem. I felt relieved after that. I know that the road to annihilating the effects of this generational curse won't wear off in one day. But with caution, consciousness, kindness, patience, and speaking and thinking positively, I would definitely get to the bottom of it no matter the situation. But don't get too carried away by the negative aspects of my parents' lives. We all fall short, and their sins are no greater than mine. And there is nothing wrong with wanting to walk in the footsteps of those you admire. However, think about how far their journey got them and how far it will get you. Imitation is the best form of flattery; being stagnant and not able to progress is not. I was able to break the curse by taking all the life lessons that the lives of my parents and relatives taught me to improve myself. Instead of doing the same exact thing they did, I took lessons from their actions. And make no mistake about it; striving to be different from everyone else wasn't easy. It is easier for one to create new habits than to break old ones. It's the same with a negative generational progression. The older ones start out their lives carelessly, not minding those coming after them. Breaking out requires a great deal of motivation and determination. It needs a great work ethic and the zeal to create a better future for yourself and your own children. Somehow, in all that darkness that haunted me from the pain and traumas of my childhood, there was always that still, small voice that made me feel understood and dignified. There was a knowing within me that I was meant for more, no matter the travails or the horrible relationship abuse. I knew that I had something different to offer the world, and I couldn't just cave in and surrender to depression, promiscuity, low self-esteem, and all the negatives associated. That voice is still with me today. I found the voice in God and also found it in the purest love of my life, my beloved husband. These voices always remind me that no matter the situation, I could never get stuck up because I am a queen, and queens don't back down; they take charge of situations. I want people to connect with this information to aid in their healing process. Escaping the confines of damaging family patterns can take various forms. But one thing is certain: countless individuals are breaking free from these patterns, often without even realizing it. A lot of individuals have been embracing their cherished childhood stories and transforming them into their own unique ventures, I am a testament to that. People are thinking about restoring what was broken in their families and strengthening the families they are creating. The tiniest step in the right direction starts with you breaking a generational curse. So, Cheers! And don't forget the most important part of it: my faith guided me through it all, the support from those who truly love me, and my perseverance which kept me focused.

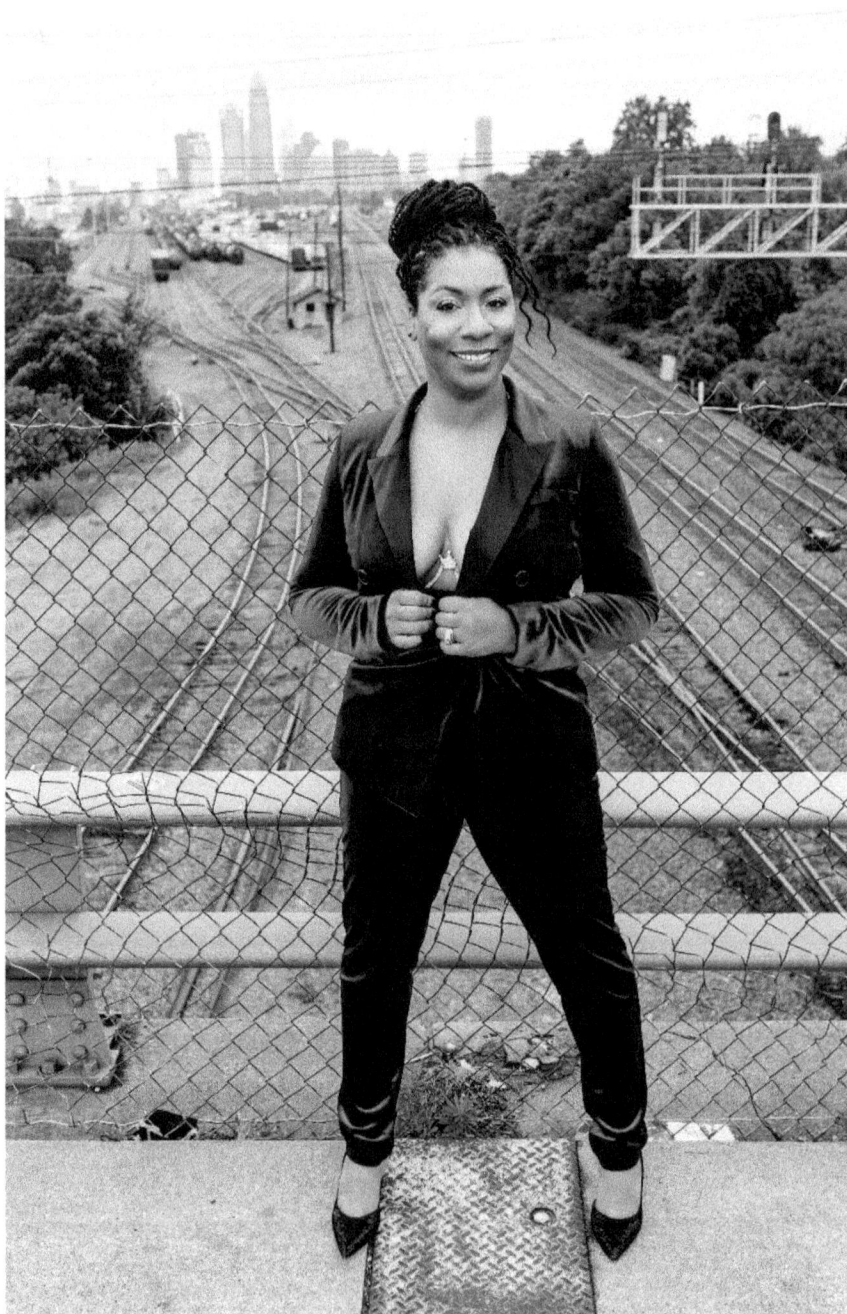

◦*◦*

CHAPTER 10

BUILD THE SEAT
AT THE TABLE

"Great things come from hard work and perseverance.
No excuses." – Kobe Bryant.

Fighting to get to the top and maintaining that position requires a great deal of perseverance. Perseverance has three aspects, and I had to hold onto all three aspects to get to where I am. Perseverance isn't all about enduring. It isn't about a show of resilience or your ability to weather tough situations. Perseverance without hope for a change of situation can make one feel lost or left behind. It can turn one into a very bitter person. The first part of persevering is your ability to stay patient. After taking stock of my life and making a conscious decision to break every barrier that would've limited me from chasing my dreams and owning my path in life, I had to learn the art of patience. Life isn't going to throw strawberries at you. Hell no! If you ever want to build your seat at the table, forget everything about a strawberry and a pink Friday kind of life. It takes patience to weather through the harsh realities of life. I have come to understand that from the start of human life, we are taught the lesson of patience through perseverance. The timeline of human pregnancy is something to ponder about. Most of us wait at least nine months in our mother's womb. And after coming into the world, we wait a few more years until we are fully developed with speech and motor skills. All through this process, we are patient with ourselves, and the people around us are equally patient, watchfully cheering us up when we fall. Don't be in a rush to attain success. I knew that fighting the pain from childhood trauma was going to take a while. I knew that studying and reinventing myself would require long hours of solitude accompanied by self-reflection. True success isn't achieved overnight. What patience does to our personalities is that it molds us correctly; it helps us shed the skin of self-doubt, mistakes, trauma, pride, deceit, and anything that isn't good for us when we finally get to the table. The table is a destination for glory. If you fail to handle your glory well, you may be pushed off the table by hands stronger than you. So, patience stirs up that spirit of humility within us, thereby helping us to be more open to learning. Patience is the greatest aspect of perseverance. It brings the greatest tranquility as it teaches the greatest lessons. The more you stay patient, the more life reveals itself to you and you, and you get surprised at the turnout of many events. I learned quickly that there are days where I could have everything all figured out and put together. And there are days when everything spells failure, disappointment, and backwardness from the first hour of the morning. What did I do in such situations? I held on. I stayed strong. Somehow, I had an assurance in God that one day everything was going to be all right. As a growing Christian, I became more serious with God after making up my mind to study. I wasn't the best Christian there was, but yes there was enough grace to pull me through. When you have God on your side, you can never give up. There are many Bible stories that can give us inspiration. One of my favorite stories is that of Joseph. It's ironic that, unlike me, Joseph had a great childhood. He was the son of his father's favorite wife and was equally the most loved son. His father, Jacob, cherished him in a way that made his siblings envious of his coat of many colors. However, when he became a teenager, his life took an ugly turn until about the age of thirty. Joseph was sold into slavery. He was falsely accused by Potiphar's wife and cast into a dungeon. But he stayed patient. In the end, he sat at the table with the king of his time. The waiting season is a significant period in the life of every human. Only a few people narrowly escape waiting for something. But many successful people passed through situations that made them second-guess their charisma and question their faith, their values, and the inspiration that they had before embarking on the journey. To bake good bread, you simply must wait for it to rise. The second aspect of perseverance that helped me through my journey was hard work. Waiting without putting in the effort is quite meaningless. What was all that waiting for if you weren't putting in the work? If you weren't striving, even slowly, to make some progress. As a girl without a mother, my support system was different. And so, I had to pat myself on the back, roll up my sleeves, and get into the mud. It is hard work that gives meaning to perseverance. In turn, hard work produces the third aspect of perseverance: Hope. While waiting, stay working. When you stay working, you have hope that the future is going to get better. I recall countless nights spent burning the midnight oil, pouring over books, and researching relentlessly. Every sacrifice I made, every ounce of effort I put in, was driven by my commitment to achieve my goals. It was my second year in graduate school when I learned I was pregnant with my second child. It was only three weeks after him that I was enrolled in another class. I refused to let setbacks define me or deter me from my path. The desire to just finish was solely up to me. And I did it. There is evidence of hard work, diligence, and commitment. Studying aggressively to improve myself and gain better learning experiences and skills promoted me amongst my peers. It boosted my confidence, albeit I was still humble. It made me realize that this woman could achieve anything. The only limitations we place on our minds are the limitations we accept and let thrive within us. We are so powerful, more than we can even imagine. But the desire to be great isn't enough. You must work the work and not focus on talking the talk. To earn your place at any table in any sphere of life, you must be ready to sacrifice your time, pleasures, and comfort. This requires a mix of patience, hard work, resilience, the right attitude, and consistency. The very first step is to set a plan. This means having a clear picture of what a successful life looks like to you and putting together a well-defined set of goals to get you that life. Planning well starts with figuring out what you want and writing it down in detail. Every right-thinking person, even with the tiniest drop of esteem, has a goal in life. To fulfill my own goal, I had no choice but to embrace hard work. I knew from the start that sitting pretty and idle wouldn't take me far or an inch close to the table. The table is meant for hard workers. Even those who cut corners put in a lot of effort to cut those corners. I had been given a second chance at life, as God spared my life. I had to use it quite wisely. I had to think of the right and best ways to put my life to good use, fulfill my dreams, bring peace to my society, and give back to the earth. Respecting this God-given chance meant that I had to work hard. I learned in my journey never to cower in the face of failure. Failure is natural. We must not fear it but find new ways to understand why we failed in that area. The best courage is accepting defeat and then striving towards victory. Merely noting where you failed is futile. When I failed at times, I never stopped working hard. I had to believe in myself and try until I achieved my dream. We can all work hard towards a great future if we have the determination and focus. Concentrating on your work and being passionate about it is very important. If one concentrates fully while working, the work gets finished successfully and very soon. It is imperative that we strive to enhance our level of concentration. While dedication and diligence play a pivotal role in nurturing our concentration prowess. Apart from my own story, I find immense joy and admiration in the stories of African American individuals who have become beacons of inspiration through their unwavering resilience. The power of perseverance and how it has shaped the lives of remarkable individuals such as Oprah, Taraji, Sheryl Lee Ralph, Fantasia, Jennifer Hudson and Sarah Jakes Roberts, just to name a few. They are in the spotlight today because of their hard work and perseverance. We all have a story to tell. And in the midst of their stories, you'll always find something that they found difficult to overcome. But their challenges weren't their end point, or the definition of their story. It was simply the start of a great story. Oprah Winfrey's success story is unique, and I can relate to some aspects because of my painful childhood. From a very young age, she experienced a level of adversity and poverty that most people would struggle to overcome. She was born into poverty and a broken home in rural Mississippi. Her parents were just 18 and 19 when they had her; and split soon after she was born. This led to her being taken in by her grandmother. And her grandmother was not your typical warm and fuzzy grandmother. No, she was a hardnosed grandmother with extremely firm hands meant for discipline. But the poverty and disciplined lifestyle didn't last forever, as she moved back with her mother at the age of six. Oprah would then experience sexual assault at an early age by some of her family members. The rounds of emotional, physical, sexual, and verbal abuse were the premise for her risky teenage behaviors. Her story is about struggle, adversity, and tragedy. But, regardless of all her unfortunate experiences, she decided to turn her life around after she lost her baby. So, she committed herself to getting an education, becoming her best, and going after her dreams. She decided to start trusting herself again, loving herself, and making choices that would improve her life rather than destroy it. In the end, she is one of the most successful women at the table. It wasn't an easy ride, but she went after the storm and found herself a reward. To be successful, you must work hard. Achievements without hard work are impossible. An idle person can never gain anything if they sit and wait for a better opportunity to come. A person who works hard can gain success and happiness in life. Nothing is easy to achieve in life without doing hard work. Failures are sometimes a part of the journey to success, but at the end of the day, it is all about how hard you have worked on the right thing, and this will get you closer to your goal. Most successful individuals had put in enough productive work before they received success in return. Just by working hard on what you believe in, you can understand its true value. That's when you start to respect the work itself and when you start to learn important life lessons. You learn to appreciate all you have, but in the meantime, you learn to be patient, take action instead of waiting, and to take responsibility for anything you have or don't have in your life. I learned that hard work plays a great role in the journey to the table. Hard work makes it easier for you to overcome procrastination, insecurities, fear of failure, and bad habits, and gives you a purpose. There is nothing else that brings more results and progress on a consistent basis than hard work. The action leads to more action. At any moment of the day, you are building and making sure that your journey continues. When you see the results of your own work, you feel grateful, accomplished, and truly satisfied with what you are doing. That makes the entire process enjoyable, and you find the strength to persevere. Never doubt the power and necessity of hard work. Create your strategy, make your plan, and take the first step toward success today! My story is a story of grass to grace. It is a story of pain to triumph. David was just a forgotten little shepherd when God prompted Samuel to ask Jesse if there was anyone left. He was anointed; hence, he rose to become King (1Samuel 16:13). I once experienced a place where I thought my potential was being wasted, but I later realized that God was actually molding me for the next level. Your current status may not appear rosy or bright. But don't draw conclusions about your case, instead learn to rely on God and his promises. Always believe in yourself, and whenever you want to give up, perhaps success is very close by. Always remember that you can achieve anything you put in your mind to achieve. My progression in my journey towards a seat at my own table isn't meant for boasting. The table that I can build myself with my own blood, sweat and tears. I will let no man take my crown (Revelation 3:11). The journey to her crown is to inspire even just one mind out there; that it is possible to hope in the midst of restoration; it is possible to sow when you don't understand the season; it is possible to live, breathe, and dream again. Honey, why don't you give yourself another chance? As David claimed the opportunity for recognition, you should be doing so. Without taking the opportunity to slay Goliath, his recognition would've been delayed. Respond to those emails now! Send out those applications! Move on to the next project! Don't let depression and disappointment turn you into a couch potato. Stand up and keep walking, even if that's all you have to do. I believe in you. I believe in the power of your dreams. I believe that you have what it takes to march toward the table and get the benefits of respect. I believe that, just like me, you can stay strong in the storm and be the epitome of perseverance.

"I can do all things through Christ who strengthens me."

(Philippians 4:13)

ACKNOWLEDGEMENTS

To my husband Chris, with love overflowing, I want to express my deepest gratitude. You have been more than just a partner; you are my ride-or-die, my rock, and my confidant. You have stood by my side through thick and thin, supporting and encouraging me to share my story with the world. We are on the same page, and for that, I am thankful. Thankful that God brought you into my life.

Dad, honor thy mother and father and thy days will be long is what resonates when I think of you. Thanks for raising me, through hardships and triumphs, your love, guidance, and support has been the foundation of my journey. You have taught me that forgiveness is a great form of love.

To my beloved children, you are my greatest blessings. Never forget the potential that lies within you. Strength is in your bloodline. You fill my heart with immense joy and love, and I will forever cherish being your mom.

I love you all always, and forever.

REFERENCES

Harder, Debra Lew. (January 15, 2919). The Story Behind the African American Spiritual Th at Evokes the Cry of The Motherless Child. Retrieved from: Wrti.org

SAMHSA. Recognizing and Treating Child Traumatic Stress. (April 21, 2022). Substance Abuse and Mental Health Services Administration. Retrieved from: www.samhsa.gov.

Scheinbaum, Chase. (April 4, 2017). At What Age Do Childhood Memories Start? Earlier than you might think. Retrieved from Fatherly.com

The Guardian. Maya Angelou quotes: 15 of the best. Wikipedia. (2023). Perseverance.

ABOUT THE AUTHOR

Erika R. Paige, the ultimate multitasker: a wife, a mom, and an entrepreneur extraordinaire. When the world was hit by the 2020 Pandemic, this superwoman didn't just sit around twiddling her thumbs. No way! She channeled her inspiration from her amazing family and unleashed her inner wordsmith, cracking open her creativity to give us not just one, but two fantastic children's books – "Gigi's Glimpse of Virtual Learning" and "Zeke's Great Imagination." Erika also developed a digital magazine entitled: "Empowered Magazine" which shines a light on authors, entrepreneurs, artists, and advocates. Erika even created "On the Same Paige Podcast" which she co-hosts with her husband Chris as they take a deeper dive into relationship issues. Erika lives in the vibrant city of Charlotte, North Carolina and is no stranger to success. Armed with a bachelor's degree from the University of Phoenix and an MBA from Fayetteville State University, she's got the beauty, and the brains to match her entrepreneurial spirit. And she certainly knows how to put those smarts to good use!

As the proud CEO of Imperfect Paige Publishing, Erika has made it her mission to empower all minds through captivating stories no matter how unique the experience. Her motto rings loud and clear to "let the world know your story."

www.ingramcontent.com/pod-product-compliance
Lightning Source LLC
Chambersburg PA
CBHW052158090426
42741CB00010B/2322